HAUNTED
MONROE COUNTY,
MICHIGAN

JERI HOLLAND

Haunted
America

Published by Haunted America
A Division of The History Press
Charleston, SC
www.historypress.com

Front cover: The William H. Boyd House, located at 405 Washington Street. The formal-style house was originally built in 1848 for Henry V. Mann, a promoter and stockholder of the Michigan and Southern Railroad, a promoter of the Monroe harbor and canal, a lawyer and Monroe County treasurer. *Photo by Jeri Holland.*
Back cover: Woodland Cemetery, located at 438 Jerome Street. Many of Monroe's earliest settlers, politicians and war combatants are buried here, including some of those who were killed during the Battle of Frenchtown in 1813. *Photo by Jeri Holland.*

First published 2023

Manufactured in the United States

ISBN 9781467147774

Library of Congress Control Number: 2023934803

Notice: The information in this book is true and complete to the best of our knowledge. It is offered without guarantee on the part of the author or The History Press. The author and The History Press disclaim all liability in connection with the use of this book.

Dedicated to
Gayle L. Tolliver
January 18, 1971–March 1, 2017

My best friend and ghost hunting partner for twenty years.

CONTENTS

CONTENTS

ACKNOWLEDGEMENTS

Rebecca Lee, MD—Thank you for double- and triple-checking my work and turning each chapter of history and facts into an enjoyable, intriguing story. You have been invaluable.

Ted and Melody, Hannah, Emily and Samuel Holland—Thank you for providing me with a home base in Monroe over the years.

Outkazt Paranormal—Thank you for letting me tag along on ghost hunts and showing the updated equipment, as I'd been out of the paranormal loop for the past few years.

INTRODUCTION

Before I tell you about how this book came to be, I first need to come clean about something. I'm not a resident of Monroe County, Michigan. Truth be told, I'm from your rival state of Ohio. Cuyahoga Falls, Ohio, to be exact.

So why, you may wonder, is an Ohioan writing a book about haunted Monroe County? I'll tell you. My cousin and his family live in Monroe, and I've always enjoyed spending time up here. In fact, if the electricity didn't go out so often, I'd move up here.

One day, I was driving around exploring some of the historic sites in Monroe. I started rattling off historic facts that I had read about, much like I would back home. I looked over at a beautiful Victorian house on Washington Street and said, "Oooo, I'll bet that house is haunted!" My twelve-year-old cousin, Hannah, asked, "When was the last time you wrote a haunted book?" I replied that I hadn't since my very first book, back in 2011. She then suggested that I write one for Monroe. Out of the mouth of babes. I thought about writing the book for a month. When I next made my way back up to my "second home" in Monroe, I brought up the subject again. My family supported the idea. I next checked with my previous editor at The History Press, and he was game. So here we are! Aside from the fun I had researching for this book, writing the book gave me a great opportunity to head north each month for extended periods of time.

I've been a self-proclaimed history geek all my life. I always loved hearing stories from my grandparents, listening to them talk about things that happened long ago. As a teen, I wondered what kind of stories my great-grandparents would share if they were around. As an adult, I embraced my love of history by working on my family tree. I found that the ghosts of my ancestors tell their stories through records and documents. What I wouldn't do to see the *actual* ghosts of my family members.

In the late '90s, I was in my late grandmother's house when I experienced the ghost of my grandfather. Several times. After that, I went on a quest to find out more about ghosts. In the year 2000, I joined a group called Spiritseekers of Ohio. I learned so much from the group. We had guest speakers teach us about photography, audio recorders and my favorite—Instrumental Trans-communication (ITC). It was during the time when digital cameras and audio recorders were becoming more commonplace, so we learned the differences between digital and analog as well. Spiritseekers had big investigations all over Ohio and beyond. It was before all the paranormal TV shows and before ghost hunting became popular, so we were shunned a lot. But that gradually lessened through the years.

I approached this book wanting to give an array of hauntings—a smorgasbord, if you will. I wanted general hauntings, with some places that could currently be investigated by most ghost hunters and some that are privately owned—not accessible to outsiders. I also wanted a few chapters with a legends-and-lore twist. Some have deep history, while in other locations, the history has been lost.

For me, one of the most rewarding parts of writing this book was researching and writing the chapter on the River Raisin National Battlefield Park. I've been interested in the park for many years and visited multiple times before I ever got any evidence. I guess they had to get to know me before they made an appearance. I only remember a couple things that happened all those years ago. One was capturing the names of soldiers on my audio recorder. There were probably a dozen names in that EVP, although I only heard about five that were crystal clear class-A EVPs. Another thing I remember was seeing a small campfire with men huddled around it. I was sitting in the truck facing the historical signs. Now that I know the history, I'm not sure why I saw that; I don't think anyone stopped near the intersection of present-day East Elm and Detroit Avenues to make a fire in hopes of warding off that freezing weather while a group of drunken Native Americans were on a rampage.

Who knows why I saw what I saw. Over the years, I have had many more experiences there. I stopped using equipment and just began using my own senses when ghost hunting. I experienced mixed feelings of despair and hatred.

Writing this book, I realized just how much of an imprint the battlefield has. I read so many personal accounts of the massacre that it left me sick. I tried to keep in the forefront of my mind that the Native Americans were furious with the incoming settlers. They felt like the white men were stealing their lands. Americans were bringing illness to them that they couldn't fight off. The Indians were losing members of their tribes left and right. They were mighty angry. It didn't help that the British helped fill them with more animosity for the newer Americans.

A few days after the massacre at River Raisin, General Proctor ordered all the townspeople to leave any remaining homes and move to Detroit. Frenchtown was left a scene of destruction and desolation. The bodies were all left where they fell. Some were buried two months later by a Kentucky cavalry regiment who retraced their steps back to Frenchtown. Most of the remains were left to be savaged by the wildlife and bleached by the sun. In the 1830s, 20-some years after the battle, some remains were taken off the battlefield and placed in military cemeteries. In the year 2000, 187 years after the battle and subsequent massacre, even more human remains were gathered up and buried in several different areas, including Memorial Place on South Monroe Street, where the Kentucky Monument stands.

After the two skirmishes, the massacre and the abandonment of bodies—how in the world will these spirits ever sleep? Today, walking on the battlefield, it surrounds me, sweeps me up into how it must have felt on those bitterly cold days in 1813.

I hope you all enjoy reading this book as much as I enjoyed researching it.

PART I
GHOSTS AMONG US

CHAPTER 1

THE BOYD HOUSE

A SPIRITED THREE-YEAR-OLD

In 1855, a merchant and Republican Party co-founder named William Boyd moved to 405 Washington Street in Monroe with his wife, Lucy, and their two young sons, Irving and Eddie. The Boyds no doubt hoped the move would be a fresh start. The first years of the couple's marriage had been inundated with heartbreak. Their oldest, William Erastmus, had died at the age of five in 1847.

Two years later, in 1857, the couple welcomed a beautiful baby girl named Clara Anna. Mr. and Mrs. Boyd were excited by the addition of a girl to the family after having had three boys. Lucy was absolutely elated and immediately commissioned girl's clothes to be made by the local seamstress. The curly-haired, bright-eyed girl was the apple of her mother's and father's eyes.

But the happiness brought about by the birth of little Clara was not to last. In 1860, tragedy arrived on the family's doorstep yet again when a scarlet fever epidemic hit Monroe County. On May 6, 1860, twelve-year-old Eddie came down with a sore throat and a headache. Two days after the lad fell ill, he developed a red, sandpaper-like rash on his stomach and a white coating over his tongue. The poor boy felt miserable. His discomfort only worsened as his fever increased. According to the mortality records, Eddie passed away on May 13, 1860.

But there was more. Immediately after Eddie's death, little Clara developed symptoms of scarlet fever. Five days later, on May 17, the precious baby girl died in the arms of her mother.

One of her parents, although it is unclear which one, wrote a beautiful, quite poetic obituary the week following:

Clara Anna Boyd Obituary
May 24, 1860
Died on Thursday morning, May 17th, Clara Anna, only daughter and youngest child of W.H. Boyd, aged 3 years.

On Sabbath previous, the oldest son Edgar Seymour, died and was buried on Monday afternoon. Both died of Scarlet Fever. The little one was at the funeral and burial of her brother, and on Tuesday went with her parents and planted with her own hands a flower on his grave—and on Friday was laid by his side, the flower still fresh on his grave. She, fair bud, beautiful and lovely, faded sooner than her flower, in Heaven to blossom.

Little Clara—Did you ever see her? Did you know her—that bright, beautiful child, with the large lustrous eyes—so ever varying in expression on—now so bewitching in their merriment; and the little face, rippling in easy arch motion, with its lips and pearly teeth and glowing cheeks and coy blushes and fitful laugh—and the long brown curls, which clustered so lovingly over her heaven-like brow and full, have concealing her little white fat neck; and her little ways, so beautifully sweet—and her little talk, so winning, so cheering, so loving, so like the music of an angel choir, and our hearts bounded within us, as we gazed and listened—and we thanked the Giver for the beautiful gift.

But earth, with all its flowers and sunlight and skylight and its winding rivers and its beauties, was not bright enough for our little Clara—and the deep tender love of idolizing parents, and the sweet love of a brother, and the endearments of home, and the homage of friends—could not keep her.

The Father in Heaven loved her with more than earthly love—and the angels loved her too, and they watched her with a heavenly care, as day by day she grew less fitted for earth, and expanded for the Bright Land—as day by day now beauties unfolded, and she seemed to clink more fondly around loving hearts, and when we were loving her the dearest, then He came—the Angel—came and bore her gently away from bleeding, breaking hearts, to the Good Shepherd who gathered her with His little Lambs.

Farewell little Clara—our sunbeam, our darling. Your little highchair, with its wee arms, sits in its accustomed corner, and your little crib stands by the bedside. Your little half worn shoes and your pretty frocks, which fall as full as they last fell over such rarely sculptured limbs, and your little books and toys, and your little dolls, with the dresses which dimpled fingers fastened there—lie awaiting you on the shelf, and there they rest.

Our little Clara will never need aught of earth again—and though her little body lies in yonder grave, over which sometimes the fireflies will light their lamps—sometimes the pale moon cast its shadow, and the violet blooms and die, and the cold snows of winter cover it—still little Clara is not there. She with "her Eddie," who awaited her on the "shining shore," are tenderly folded in the arms of Him "who doeth all things well."

William and Clara Boyd eventually welcomed a second baby girl in 1864, named Carrie Lucy. Not long after, frequent sightings of the ghostly figure of a young girl inside the Boyd House began to be reported. The sightings would continue for the next 150 years.

In 1881, the Boyds hosted a forty-five-year-old schoolteacher from Summerfield Township during the school semester. One evening, the woman was frightened "out of her skin" at a terrifyingly spooky sighting in her bedroom. A toddler, wearing a billowy dress that sat just below her knees and button-up shoes, walked across the room to look out the window. Knowing the only child that lived in the house was sixteen years old, the schoolteacher moved out without delay.

The 848 Gothic-style Boyd House located at 405 Washington Street. *Photo by Jeri Holland, 2021.*

In 1915, following the death of William and Lucy, Carrie Boyd returned to live in her childhood home. She used the downstairs parlor rooms for herself and rented out the other rooms in the house. Her renters often claimed to spot a young girl around the home. Most frequently, a boarder named Jean Comstock saw a toddler with curly brown hair wearing pantaloons—which, of course, had gone out of style by the 1920s. Perhaps, unlike other boarders, she was more accepting of the apparition, and thus Clara Anna felt welcomed to appear more often.

Carrie Boyd died in November 1949. But the sightings didn't stop then. Frequent sightings were reported by subsequent residents over the next fifty years.

The "Legend Tripping in Historic Monroe" website, owned by Chelsea Baker, tells of several additional sightings. One such story referred to a local man who claimed that as a child, his friend once saw the faint face of a little girl peeking out at him through one of the home's windows. Another sighting involved a boy named Brandon, who grew up in the home. Baker spoke to Brandon's mother-in-law, who reported that Brandon recalled often playing with a little girl in the home as a young child. The only problem? Brandon didn't have a little sister, and no one seemed to know who the girl could have been. Could Brandon's young playmate have been none other than Clara Anna Boyd?

In the 1970s, Phil Sessions, a Monroe County deputy sheriff, overheard what he thought was his two daughters laughing and giggling in their playroom. When he went to check on the girls, he found not two, but *three* little girls playing. Having spotted Sessions, his daughters' playmate rose and quickly passed into the hallway. She climbed up the stairs and disappeared. Deputy Sessions followed her and searched the upstairs, but the child was nowhere to be found.

I personally visited Monroe in 2020 and went for a walk along Washington Avenue. Having a historical interest in the home, I stopped to look at the house for myself. The homeowner was out gardening, and she stopped to talk to me. After telling me about the house, she brought up the fact that it is haunted by a little girl who died there in 1860. After asking a few questions, I learned that the homeowner herself had never encountered the ghostly Clara since buying the home in the late 1990s but her neighbors and guests had. The owner's neighbors had often reported seeing the ghost of a little girl peering out of the home's windows. When I embarked on writing this book, I just knew I had to relay the story of sweet little Clara Boyd and the haunting of the home on Washington Street.

CHAPTER 2

ANGELO'S NORTHWOOD VILLA

Nestled between Toledo and Detroit, Erie Township lies in the rural southeast corner of Monroe County. During the 1920s, one of the town's most illustrious eating establishments was known as the Villa. The restaurant was originally owned by a man named Jimmy Hayes. Known to many as "Gentleman Jimmy," Hayes was notorious for his underworld activities. During Prohibition, the Villa became a prime location for the mobster group the Purple Gang to conduct business.

Gerald James "Jimmy" Hayes was quite the businessman. He catered to every level of society by owning multiple alcohol and gambling businesses in Toledo. The Jovial Club, located at 631 St. Clair Street, was well known as the poor man's gambling establishment. It was a place where even a nickel could be wagered. Hayes also owned the Gentlemen's Club, located at 220 St. Clair Street; here, craps, roulette and other gambling ventures were available. The Buckeye Cigar Store, at 229 Superior Street, was believed to also have been owned by Hayes. It was Toledo's number-one horse-racing betting parlor.

As Hayes gained in stature, he branched out and opened the highly successful Ramona Casino in Harbor Springs, Michigan, the Hollywood Clubs in Miami and a few places in Cleveland.

In 1924, Jimmy Hayes opened the Villa just across the Michigan-Ohio state line on Dixie Highway (aka the Highway of Booze). The Villa became a haven for alcohol and gambling along with other illegal organized crime activities.

The Purple Gang, also known as the Sugar House Gang, began as a felonious mob of bootleggers and hijackers composed primarily of Jewish mobsters. They were led by the four Burnstein brothers: Raymond, Joseph, Isadore and Abraham. By the late 1920s, the Purple Gang had control over the Detroit and Toledo underworld—gambling, liquor, drugs and so on. It was during this time that the gang began its search for a new headquarters.

Erie Township's rural location provided the perfect setting and easy infiltration; there was less law enforcement than in the big cities, and the group could operate their business while having better control of the comings and goings of others. For the Purple Gang, the Villa was the perfect place from which to conduct the business of importing—or, rather, smuggling— alcohol from Canada. The smuggled alcohol was then sold throughout Michigan and Ohio.

The Villa served its purpose of headquarters well—for a time, that is. On August 15, 1924, at around midnight, Michigan State Police entered the establishment with a search warrant, seeking evidence of bootlegging and gambling. They found Jimmy Hayes guarding the staircase to the Villa's gambling room. The police forcibly entered, breaking down the front door. Many of Hayes's patrons fled through an unguarded back door to the safety of their waiting cars.

After the raid, Frank Mays, manager of the Villa, said that the Michigan State Police had confiscated $50 in cash and several slot machines. Later, the Michigan State Police reported having demolished over $2,000 in gambling machines. Law enforcement then declared that the strip of Dixie Highway north of the Ohio state line had been entirely cleansed of liquor and gambling.

Both Hayes and Mays pleaded not guilty to bootlegging and gambling. A bond of $1,000 along with a hearing date of September 12, 1924, was set. Not long after Michigan State Police raided the Villa, the front door was replaced, the damage was repaired and the Villa's patrons returned. Everything was back to "normal." Or so it seemed.

In 1926, Jimmy Hayes experienced the first attempt on his life when he was shot by unknown assailants on Jefferson Avenue and Sixteenth Street in Toledo. He wasn't killed, however, by those three slugs. Several years later, Hayes's fate was sealed on October 4, 1934, the day he was found in an alley off West Palmer Avenue in Detroit with twenty-six shotgun slugs in his body. Two men happened to be nearby when Hayes was thrown out of the car, followed by a shirt and a coat. His body was still warm.

"It was the conventional gangster ride," the Detroit police told the *Detroit Free Press* at the time. Hayes had been murdered elsewhere before his body

Angelo's Northwood Villa. *Photo by Jeri Holland, 2023.*

was dumped in the alley shortly after 8:00 a.m. that Thursday. Gamblers had gathered in Detroit for the World Series, and thus the police considered the possibility that Hayes, who was extremely wealthy and had handled big bets on the baseball game, had drawn down the enmity of other gamblers. It was and remains highly suspected that the Purples were behind the killing. The speculation is that Hayes was murdered by the Purple Gang because they were trying to take over his very successful gaming operations.

Following the death of Jimmy Hayes, his operations were taken over by underling Ed Warnke. Warnke sold the Villa in 1955, and the restaurant then became the Northwood Villa. The establishment continued to serve for decades as a supper club and upscale eatery. It closed in the early 1990s.

In 2000, the restaurant was reopened after being purchased by Angelo Tsipis. Renamed Angelo's Northwood Villa, the restaurant has seen nearly two decades of success under the current ownership. Today, Angelo's Northwood Villa has become known as one of the top restaurants of the Toledo area. The restaurant is operated by the father-and-son team of Angelo Tsipis and Alex Tsipis. The Tsipis men pride themselves on providing top-notch food, service and atmosphere in their restaurant. Much of the vintage decor is the same as it was when the Villa first opened its doors. Proudly displayed is a prominent framed picture of the Purple Gang, which hangs over a large fireplace in one of the dining rooms.

Mirrors along one wall once folded down to serve as craps tables. The ornate, inverted beveled ceiling in the center of the main dining room was once open to the second floor. Machine gun–toting guards once paced back and forth along the upper balcony, keeping tabs on the gambling below. A peephole in the ceiling once served as a spot where the owners could surreptitiously watch gambling patrons to make sure there was no funny business taking place. The beautifully refinished dance floor is original, as are the glass chandeliers. The hidden cigar room, once a hangout for the Purple Gang, is still utilized by Angelo's customers today. The restaurant basement formerly contained hidden passageways and the entrance to a tunnel system. The openings to the tunnel system have since been covered, but during Prohibition days, bootleggers would distribute smuggled liquor from Lake Erie to nearby homes and businesses through the tunnels.

Alex Tsipis, who lived above the restaurant for a few years, has said that late at night, he could often hear the clinking of glasses and people laughing

Inside the dining rooms of Angelo's Northwood Villa. The next dining area over are where two shadow men were captured on film. *Photo by Jeri Holland, 2023.*

in the dining rooms below. Since the Villa was such a favorite meeting spot for the Purple Gang, it's not hard to believe they'd want to keep the party going there into the afterlife.

A few weeks ago, I was looking for a place to have lunch. I had heard about Angelo's Northwood Villa's mob-connected past and decided to head there to take in the history of the place. After we arrived, my party and I were promptly led into the main dining room. As we were being seated, I felt a hand grab my shoulder. I looked right and I looked left, but nobody was behind me. *Hmmmm, interesting,* I thought. My family and I ordered, and we had a wonderful lunch. The atmosphere takes one back to the 1920s and '30s. It's dark, elegant and quiet.

By about the third or fourth time our waitress, Keisha, came to our table, I had decided to just come out with it. "Is this place haunted?" I asked her.

Indeed, it was, Keisha said. She began telling us things that had happened to her. Early one morning before the restaurant opened, Keisha heard her name called multiple times, and as she pointed out, her name is not common, so she did not believe these incidents to be a mere fluke. There was a time when Keisha was giving a tour of Angelo's Northwood Villa to some guests; she had explained that the joint was haunted, but her guests didn't believe her. Well, a short time later, a wine bottle flew off a shelf and crashed to the floor, startling everyone. The message was loud and clear!

Hearing these stories from Keisha, I looked over at Ted, my cousin and fellow ghost hunter, who was dining with me. I gave him a look that said, *We have to check this out!*

After sharing her experiences, Keisha retrieved a three-inch binder full of history about both the restaurant and the Purple Gang. It held much of the information shared earlier in this chapter. A short time later, a cook, Glenna, came out from the kitchen to talk to us and share her experiences. She told us of shadows that she's often witnessed moving along the dining room, but only early in the morning and late at night. (My theory on the shadows being seen only at these times is that everyone is too busy during the other parts of the day to notice them.) The other two people with us were my sister Lee Ann and cousin Melody. Both ghost-curious, they listened intently. Glenna next told us about having seen ghostly figures go through the kitchen and—one time—even through a wall. She then brought out her phone that held videos of the ghosts of a man clearly walking past the bathroom and one in the dining room. After ghost hunting for the past twenty years, I've come to doubt more than I believe if I'm not there for the actual recording. However, these videos of the capture were amazing. Glenna relayed a few more details.

This area is the spiritually active Cigar Bar at Angelo's Northwood Villa. *Courtesy of Angelo's Northwood Villa.*

A ghostly apparition is frequently spotted in the cigar room, helping himself to the goods. Sightings are so common that it's no longer frightening to the employees. Nearly every staff member of Angelo's Northwood Villa has felt touches and has seen the ghosts—and all have stuck around long term. They all agree that the ghosts are former gamblers and members of the Purple Gang lurking around, making their presence known. Or is it former owner Jimmy Hayes himself? Although he was killed in Detroit, it is said that he was most comfortable at the Villa.

I plan to head back in a few weeks, and I can't wait. Go check it out at 6630 South Dixie Highway in Erie. The employees at Angelo's Northwood Villa love to answer any questions about their experiences in the building. For anyone over forty-five, make sure you have a flashlight on your phone so you can see the menu in the darker 1930s atmosphere. Then sit back, relax and check out your surroundings.

CHAPTER 3

THE *GRAY GHOST*

Within weeks of the start of Prohibition on January 17, 1920, the organized smuggling of imported whiskey, rum and other liquor to the Great Lakes from Canada—known as "rumrunning"—had begun. Lake Erie's famous phantom, the aptly named *Gray Ghost*, was one such rumrunner. The *Gray Ghost* was known for its sturdiness and speed, making it one of the most sought-after prizes by Prohibition enforcers. The ship's top speed of over thirty-nine knots, even when fully loaded, was credited in several narrow escapes from capture.

Lee Leonard of Green Bay, Wisconsin, was a skipper of several rumrunner vessels, including the *Gray Ghost*. In October 1929, in Cleveland, Leonard was arrested by the U.S. Coast Guard as he attempted to heist a cabin cruiser filled to the gills with liquor. Freed on bond, he was ordered to appear in court on February 5, 1930. He didn't show.

The last purported sighting of Lee Leonard was on the night of January 7, 1930. An Erieau, Ontario hotel manager swore he spotted Leonard depart from the hotel to board a ship named the *Gray Ghost*. M.K. Jackson, a sub-collector of customs for Erie, reported that the *Gray Ghost* had cleared the port on the night of January 7 with 125 cases of whiskey aboard. He stated that a "Lee Edwards" (Leonard's usual alias) had signed the customs manifesto as the skipper. The *Gray Ghost* and its three crewmates had been sent along their way from Erieau. Neither ship nor crew ever reached any of their suspected smuggling destinations of Monroe, Michigan; Sandusky, Ohio; or Cleveland, Ohio.

It wasn't long before hair-raising tales of the *Gray Ghost*'s wanderings flitted about Lake Erie. Just weeks later, in late January 1930, the ship was allegedly spotted cruising under a full moon offshore Monroe, Michigan, close enough to the coast for one to read the vessel's now-infamous name on the port side of the ship. According to the *Sandusky Register* newspaper, a boat captain off the shore of Monroe spotted the *Gray Ghost* and also what appeared to be a lone occupant sitting upright and frozen to death.

Two days later, another report to law enforcement came in that the *Gray Ghost* had been seen directly off the shore of Pelee Island. Pilot Jerry Fitten, of the Leamington-Pelee Island Air Mail, subsequently cruised the vicinity where the sighting had been made but failed to uncover a single sign of the *Gray Ghost*. John W. Parker, the Erie County, Ohio sheriff, known as the "Flying Sheriff," also spent two hours in the air attempting to locate the vessel. Despite clear weather and flying low, he was unable to find any trace of a ship—phantom or otherwise. A short time later, *Gray Ghost* was reported to have been seen nearly 150 miles across Lake Erie, haunting the Port Stanley region.

In February 1930, a Cleveland mother by the name of Alice Seculick called Sheriff Parker and reported her son Joe Meyers was missing. The last time she spoke with him was January 7, right before he boarded *Gray Ghost*. He had said he was making his way on through several Lake Erie ports and would return to Sandusky in a few days. Sheriff John Parker, Joe Esch and an unnamed Canadian man from Leamington went on an air search once again. However, not one of the aviators found any trace of the *Gray Ghost* or its crew.

In March 1930, two boys were playing on Orchard Beach near Sandusky, Ohio, when a surf-torn body came ashore. It was that of Joe Meyers, the *Gray Ghost*'s pilot.

By 1931, the *Gray Ghost* had been spotted in the grim darkness near Ashtabula and Conneaut. A year later, it had appeared yet again off the waterfront of Monroe County, Michigan. Then, the crew of the freighter *Fellowcraft* reportedly came across the ghostly vessel while transporting automobile parts from Cleveland to Detroit, but upon arrival back in Sandusky, no crew member would utter a word about the encounter. It wasn't until over a year later when one of the crew was quoted as saying, "Ol' *Gray Ghost* was bouncing up and down behind great throws of spray as she shot along like nothin'."

In the April 1932 edition of the *Port Clinton Herald and Republican*, a Sandusky fisherman reported seeing the eerie ship riding white-tipped breakers. The

Looking out at Lake Erie, you can imagine the rumrunning that escaped the clutches of law enforcement, the ships and even unknown serpents. *Photo by Lee Ann Bennett in Luna Pier.*

next day, the same newspaper reported that two bodies had been found on the lakeshore. Dr. A.B. Grierson, Erie County coroner, believed the two were *Gray Ghost* victims.

In subsequent years, other veteran fishermen were quoted in the *Tribune* as having said the "spook ship" had been seen bouncing up and down in the spray as it whistled along the water at an almost unbelievable speed.

While reading of these purported ghost ship encounters, what makes a phantom ship, you might ask?

In the 1940s, Ralph De S. Childs, an authority on phantom ships and professor of humanities at the Cooper Union for the Advancement of Science and Art, posited that five qualities distinguish ghost ships from real ships. "All you must do to tell whether a vessel is a ghost ship or a real one is to apply five simple tests. They have a common behavior," Childs said. "One is, they tend to sail against the wind or at high speed with no wind at all. The second is, they have no crews, or their crews are statue-like and inactive. A third test is that several phantoms are fire ships. Fourth, they are prone to reappear on fixed dates after suffering disaster. And fifth, some seem under the age-old curse of never making port," Childs said in a published journal article titled "Phantom Ships."

The appropriately named *Gray Ghost* meets several of these criteria: it has been repeatedly spotted traveling at an astonishing speed; it is sighted only at night and without a crew (save one occasion); and finally, it has never been seen making port.

Perhaps you can spot the *Gray Ghost* while standing on the shore of Luna Pier or while camping at Sterling State Park or Safe Harbor Toledo Beach, all locations of previous sightings.

CHAPTER 4

THE VANISHING HITCHHIKER

The elusive hitchhiker story is a pervasive urban legend. It is woven, in various forms, into frightening tales of local lore all over the country. Monroe County has its own version, set in Raisinville, Michigan. The only difference in the one told here—it's true.

For as long as anyone in the area can remember, drivers have reported sightings of an older man walking along a specific county road. Some motorists have even stopped to pick up the man. He always, however, ends up disappearing before reaching their destination.

It sounds like an exceptional story, one perhaps concocted to give delightful shudders to small children huddled together around a campfire. This story, however, might be more truth than legend, and the ghost might be more paranormal than fictional.

Most commonly, motorists report having encountered a forty- to fifty-year-old man on Nichols Road. He is said to have gray hair and is usually described as having a white beard and dressed in overalls. Sometimes he has been wearing an overshirt or jacket; in some instances, the jacket was worn, and other times it was slung over his arm. Most times he has appeared as a solid form to passersby, but others have reported that he appeared somewhat transparent throughout the entire encounter.

Christopher Woahmer was a Raisinville-area farmer who lived in the late nineteenth century. By all accounts, Woahmer was a man quite fond of the drink. Much to his wife's dismay, Woahmer was known to go on benders where he'd accomplish much more drinking than farmwork. Sometimes the benders lasted all week long. It was during these periods that the outdoor chores fell on Mrs. Woahmer. By the end of the bender, she'd be fed up and, as one can imagine, would stew for days. Invariably, once Woahmer ran out of booze, he'd spend days in bed recovering. Mrs. Woahmer would let him have it, and he'd have no choice but to lay there and listen. Decades upon decades of this behavior passed. Mrs. Woahmer had had enough.

One day, after a particularly long bender, Mrs. Woahmer decided to teach her husband a lesson. She slipped carbolic acid into his stew—not enough to kill him, mind you. Just enough to make him miserable. It worked; Christopher Woahmer had such a stomachache! He knew he had to get to the doctor to make the miserable stomach cramping and intense vomiting stop. He went out to get his wagon hitched up. Only problem was he had forgotten to fix it the week prior. Woahmer then went to the barn to fetch his horse. After struggling to get its harness on, he found Old Buck with a swollen, lame front foot. So off he went afoot—first on present-day South Custer Road. From there he took present-day Lewis Avenue toward Ida, where a physician lived in town. He never made it. Woahmer was found the next day on the side of the road—frozen to death where he fell.

Even today, 140 years later, Christopher Woahmer is still trying to get to the doctor. In the past, when hitchhiking was common, there were often reports of people picking up an elderly man who requested to go to Ida. The Good Samaritans would take him all the way into the rural community of Ida, only to find him no longer in their car.

Nowadays, picking up hitchhikers seems to mostly be a thing of the past, but that doesn't mean Woahmer isn't still trying to make his way to medical attention.

According to the newspaper *Crawford Avalanche*, one cold wintry night in 1990, Christina Taylor was driving with her mother in the car. Driving a straightaway, she and her mother saw a man walking along the remote country road. She couldn't stop, however, because the narrow road was too ice-covered to safely do so. They passed the man and could hear another vehicle behind them. Christina's mother said, "Let's turn around and pick him up; it's too cold for that old man."

Christina dutifully turned around, and they collected the elderly gentleman. After he got into the car, they asked him where he was headed. He said, "To the doctor at Ida." Christina's mother said, "I don't recall there being a doctor there." The man responded with, "Miss, I'm really sick."

Christina later recalled he was an old man with white hair, dressed entirely in denim.

When they got to Ida, Christina turned around to let him know they were there. There was no one in the back seat. There had been no stops. In fact, she had never even slowed down until reaching Ida's main intersection. He couldn't have left the car—and yet, he was gone.

A man with a similar story was a local farmer. One night, the farmer and his son came across an older man walking along the road. The driver rolled down his window and offered a ride to the man he thought looked to be a fellow farmer. The farmer told the old man to jump up on his tailgate and he'd drop him off at Ida on his way to Toledo. Upon reaching the small community, the driver pulled over and turned around to make sure the man had jumped off the tailgate. There was no one there.

Is the vanishing man Christopher Woahmer? Sure sounds like it, but I can't say for sure. If you're driving along that stretch between Raisinville and Ida, keep your eyes open. You may spot an old farmer walking along the road, trying to thumb a ride.

CHAPTER 5
REMEMBER THE RAISIN!

By January 1813, the War of 1812 was well underway. The previous year, long-existing tensions among the Americans, the British and various Indigenous peoples had finally boiled over into war. The principal belligerents, the Americans and the British, had both aligned themselves with various Native American peoples in an attempt to settle, once and for all, conflicts stemming from northwestern territorial expansion.

The Battles at Frenchtown took place in present-day Monroe, Michigan, over a several-day period in January 1813. The Native Americans were led by two Wyandot chiefs and consisted of braves from the Shawnee, Potawatomi, Ottawa, Chippewa, Delaware, Miami, Winnebago, Creek, Sauk and Fox peoples. There is so much history to be explored regarding the Battles at Frenchtown. This chapter won't delve too far into the history, however, as those details are readily available elsewhere online and in the local museums. Instead, this chapter will concentrate on the bloody horrors of the January 23 massacre—and its aftermath.

The first Frenchtown battle took place on January 18, 1813. American lieutenant colonel William Lewis led his forces in a charge across the frozen River Raisin to attack the British and Indian camp. The estimated total casualties for that battle were approximately thirty killed and sixty wounded.

The second skirmish at Frenchtown happened before dawn on January 22, 1813. It lasted all of twenty minutes. The ill-prepared Americans lost 397 soldiers, and 547 more were taken prisoner. When it was over, the Americans had surrendered to the British and Native Americans. British colonel Henry Proctor ordered American general James Winchester—captured during this stage of the battle—to carry a flag of truce to his men. Winchester agreed on one condition—his forces would surrender only if their injured would be transported to Fort Malden, located in present-day Amherstburg, Ontario.

A battle participant, Private Thomas Dudley, was present for the terms of the American surrender, in which it was agreed that the wounded Americans would be taken to Fort Malden. All of the wounded would be cared for by the British—the Native Americans were not to handle the wounded.

The British wasted no time in collecting their own wounded, along with some Americans who were readily ambulatory, and headed back to Fort Malden. The plan was to return for the non-ambulatory American soldiers later, and several British troops were left to guard the prisoners. Ultimately, however, the British failed to gather the wounded and unprotected Americans. Several Frenchtown residents from a line of homes along present-day Elm Road took some of the injured American soldiers into their homes. Others were not so fortunate and lay on the snowy ground for the next twenty-four hours, too far gone to be given aid.

For the abandoned, wounded Americans, the cold night of January 22 was long and harsh. As the dawn of Saturday, January 23, approached, however, the situation was about to get even worse. A large group of renegades was making its way toward Frenchtown.

According to eyewitnesses, about two hundred renegades spent the early hours of January 23 imbibing from barrels of whiskey given to them by British Colonel Proctor. The few British guards left to guard the Americans could not prevent what happened next. The Native Americans attacked. They set fire to the buildings that housed any of the wounded. As the Potawatomi marched prisoners north toward Detroit, they killed any who could not keep their pace. According to an account from a survivor in Glenn Clift's book *Remember the Raisin!*, "The road was for miles strewed with the mangled bodies."

Private Thomas Dudley reported what happened next:

> *The Native Americans entered a house where many of the wounded officers were staying. In the cellar, there were several barrels of alcohol from which they drank. The renegades then came back upstairs to where Dudley and three other officers were staying. Captain* [Paschal] *Hickman, confined to his bed due to his wounds, was tomahawked in front of* [Dudley].

The following are some firsthand and secondhand accounts of that morning:

On the next day after the battle on the said River Raisin, a short time after sunrise, [Joseph Robert] saw the Indians kill the American prisoners, with their tomahawks, and that they shot several—that the Indians set the houses on fire, so that in going out the prisoners were massacred and killed as aforesaid; that is to say 3 were shot, others were killed in the houses, and burnt with the houses. The Indians burnt first the house of Jean Baptite Jereaume, and afterwards that of Gabriel Godfrey, Jr. [Joseph Robert] was informed that there were about 48 or 49 prisoners in the two houses. [Robert saw] dead bodies on the highway [North Dixie Highway] which the hogs were tearing and eating. Mr. Brunot told [Robert] that the Indians had killed those of the prisoners who were least wounded, & that the others were burnt alive.

Antoine Cuiellerie and Alexis Salliot reported that two prisoners have been burnt in the Gandon's house. The Native Americans tore out the hearts of the prisoners and had brought them still smoking into the houses yet to be burned.

The Indians fired on a man named Solo, son-in-law to Stephen Lebeau, when he fled from the Gandon's house to that of Lebeau saying he was mortally wounded, shared the Richmond Enquirer *on April 9th, 2013. Stephen Lebeau placed Solo on his bed, but he died in the process. An Indian knocked on the door and Lebeau, having opened the door, received a bullet to his chest and died.*

Private Hamilton, with the Kentucky volunteers, shared that as the Indians led prisoners away from Frenchtown, they first came across a man who had been set afire and was expiring quickly. One of the Indians kicked at the ashes on the man's back and said, "damn'd son of a bitch."

From Antoine Boalard's account:

The next day after the last battle on River aux Raisins, he saw the Indians kill the Secretary of the American General, who was on the horse of the Indian who had taken him prisoner, with a rifle shot; that the prisoner fell on one side, and an Indian came forward with a sabre, finished him, scalped him, stripped him and carried away his clothes. The body remained two days on the highway [South Dixie Highway]…and was part eat up by the hogs.

The south end of the battlefield where the homes of Frenchtown once sat. *Photo by Samuel D. Holland.*

Afterwards with Peter Audrain, Francois Lasselle, Hubert Lecroix, Charles Chovin, and Louis Lajoye, took up the corpse at dusk of the evening, and carried it into a field near the woods, where hogs did not go. They dared not to bury it in fear of being surprised by the Indians.

From Peter Audrain, February 5, 1813:

I hereby certify that the next day after the last battle at the River aux Raisins, the Secretary of the American General was taken near the door of the deponent—was wounded and placed on a horse, that seven or eight Indians were near the house, one of whom shot him in the head with a rifle—that he did not fall off his horse, until another Indian drawing his sabre, struck him on the head several times, and then he fell to the ground; was scalped and stripped of this clothes, and left on the road where he remained one day and a half; I the deponent with Francois Lasselle, Hubert LaCroix and Louis Chovin, on the evening of the second day took up the body, carried it to the skirt of the woods and covered it with a few branches, but could not stay to bury it, for fear of the Indians that were in the neighborhood; that on the next day after the last battle, I was near the house of Gabriel Godfrey Jr., and the house of Jean Baptiste Gere somewhere a great number of prisoners were collected, and that I heard the screaming of the prisoners whom the Indians were tomahawking; that the savages set the house on fire and went off.

The south end of the River Raisin National Battlefield Park. *Photo by Jeri Holland.*

From Alexis Labadie, February 6, 1813:

> *I certify that the bodies of the Americans, killed at the battle of la riviere aux Raisins, of the 22nd of January last, and the day after remain unburied, and that I have seen the hogs and dogs eating them.*
>
> *The hogs appeared to be rendered mad by a diet of Christian flesh. I saw the houses of Mr. Gereanme and Mr. Godfrey on fire; and have heard there were prisoners in them. The inhabitants did not dare to bury them, on account of the Indians. The inhabitants have been threatened by the Indians if they did not take up arms against the Americans.*

Several personal accounts were shared with the newspaper *Lancaster Intelligence* on March 13, 1813:

> *On the morning of the 23rd about sunrise, a large body of Indians came, plundered the wounded of their clothing, and every thing of value, and [they] tomahawked and scalped all that were unable to march; among whom were some valuable officers, particularly Captain [Paschal]*

Hickman. The remainder were taken prisoners, as they termed it; and many are either killed or are still in their possession. Our loss is estimated at about 200 killed. The loss of the enemy could not be ascertained.

Needless to say, this blood-stained ground is forever embedded with the horrors that took place on it. The moment you arrive at the River Raisin Battlefield National Park, you feel as though you've stepped back in time. These battlefields, which encompass the areas around East Elm Avenue and North Dixie Highway, are known as some of the most haunted in America. The spirits of the dead are believed to still linger on the ground by the River Raisin, casualties of some of the bloodiest fighting of the War of 1812.

With so much fear, death, destruction, suffering and sorrow concentrated in one area, it's no wonder that so many visitors and locals have reported being able to feel, hear and see odd phenomena while walking the trails of the battlefield. Any given day, a visitor just might encounter some strange activity—equipment malfunctions, the sounds of soldiers crying out or

The annual Prisoner of War and Missing in Action (POW/MIA) Trail of Remembrance Memorial display alongside the River Raisin Battlefield Trail. *Photo by Jeri Holland.*

POW/MIA Recognition Day is commemorated on the third Friday of September each year. *Photo by Jeri Holland.*

ghostly apparitions—as many soldiers are said to still haunt the place where they spent the final moments of their curtailed lives. The tragic impressions of that day seem to linger. It seems that no matter how many visitors roam the battlefield on any given day, it remains quiet, eerie.

According to eyewitnesses, the sounds of gunfire and the smell of gunpowder can be experienced when no one is in the area. Once, a visitor to the battlefield reported seeing several men marching through the tall grass along Detroit Avenue. He thought they were reenactors—until they vanished into thin air.

Chase Blackwell shared his story with me in Facebook's Haunted Monroe, Michigan group:

> *When I was a young boy I was living on the core of the battlefield. It was midnight, I was eating dinner when I looked up in the window right across from me. I saw a full apparition of a Kentucky militiaman. He had all the equipment on the black uniform with the red fringe and a brick red knapsack. He had his musket or rifle on his shoulder. At first, he did not notice me but then after a few seconds he stopped and turned and looked at*

me for a long time. It felt as if he had seen a long-lost friend. I felt as if I understood his unspoken thoughts. He suddenly turned and I quickly turned my head away. When I looked back up, he was gone. I later learned that I have three or four relatives that fought in the battles and witnessed the massacre. Three of my relatives buried the dead in 1813.

A few people shared their accounts on Facebook's Haunted Monroe, Michigan page. Kathy Drake visited the battlefield park with her husband and described the experience as this: "[I] definitely heard either drumming or maybe gunfire. 'Rat-a-tat-tat, rat-a-tat-tat.' I said, 'What is that?' My husband replied, 'Nothing. Let's go.'"

Joyce Barronton heard faint cannon fire in the distance while walking the battlefield.

Laura Lamkin said, "Look...that place...you can't even walk through there without feeling the eyes staring at you. My oldest said the same thing when he rode his bike to Pilot [gas station] one night....But it's an eerie vibe you get. And you really feel like you're being stared down...you just can't see what's staring at you."

A local ghost-hunting group out of Toledo and southeast Michigan called Outkazt Paranormal regularly spends a few hours at night on the River Raisin Battlefield with their collection of equipment. The group has been going there since 2015, although a few members have been going longer. They have a range of ghost-detecting equipment, but their go-to is the Olympus recorders and two spirit boxes: the P-SB7T and P-SB7 ITC Research Boxes. With this equipment, they've captured both residual and intelligent responses.

Melissa Owens, lead investigator and EVP (electronic voice phenomena) analyst, shared some of Outkazt Paranormal's best EVPs they've captured over the years.

These were taken at the fork in the trail, behind what would have been homes in 1813.

- "You look like a coward."
- "Am I dead?"
- "You know what I regret..."
- "I'm Marshall," and thirteen seconds later, "Marshall."
- "Hide the body." Remember, the American soldiers attempted to hide the bodies in the woods from the pigs but didn't have time to bury them because of the Native Americans tomahawking and scalping those left alive.

- "Will you help me?"
- "Does one of you have a gun?"
- "George and I are having a baby," said with a southern accent and perfectly clear.

These next EVPs are from the field behind the pavilion, straight across from the parking area off 1403 Elm Avenue:

- "Christ."
- "Help me."
- "Zachary, please," and twenty-three seconds later, "Zachary."
- "I love you, Melissa."

This was recorded at the back at the end of the trail near Mill Street.

- "Lieutenant!"

These were taken at the pavilion with two members of Outkazt present:

- "Satan."
- "Proctor." Is this referring to British colonel Henry Procter?

Behind the pavilion, close to the wood line, the following were recorded:

- "They're coming."
- "Rape," and thirty seconds later, "Women rape."
- "Bury him."

Outkazt Paranormal investigated several of the homes along Elm Avenue before they were purchased from the River Raisin Battlefield National Park and torn down. They had fantastic luck in capturing EVPs in real time, through the spirit box and on audio recorders:

- "Daddy, help me."
- "Move out the way."
- "Leave it alone."
- "Go behind them."

Although these are the best EVPS captured, there are countless others and many experiences of footsteps, coughing, crying, screaming, gunfire and more. Melissa, from Outkazt Paranormal, has also experienced seeing a female apparition dressed in white and several soldiers walking south. Another time, she felt an overwhelming sense of sadness overtake her for about ten minutes.

I personally have been going to the battlefield for about fifteen years and have experienced the paranormal of the blood-soaked land. On one of my favorite trips to the battlefield, I took my young cousins to our annual visit to the former museum on East Elm. After watching the film portraying the battles, I asked the ranger if he'd had any ghostly sightings. He gave me the usual national park spiel about how they leave the spirits to themselves and

A house on East Elm Avenue, a section of the original Frenchtown. The house inhabitants experienced TVs and lights turning off and on, doors slamming and more. One evening, bloodcurdling screams were recorded with a digital audio recorder. This house and neighboring homes were purchased by the National Park Service and torn down to expand the River Raisin National Battlefield Park. *Courtesy of Melissa Owens.*

"nothing happens here." As I was walking into the restroom, I spotted a sign that said "Caution: Hand dryer may turn on by itself." *Hmmm, okay.* Years prior to that visit, I asked a volunteer the same question. She shared that the lights would go on and off and the back-door alarm would go off for no rhyme or reason.

Whenever I stay in Monroe, I try to get out to the battlefield once or twice during the quiet of the night. Once there, I make the typical move when ghost hunting—I turn on my audio recorder and begin asking questions. Some of my most memorable ones that I recall are:

- "What's your name?" "Joseph...William, Samuel...Cyrus."
- "Why are you here?" "We gotta go."
- Multiple "Help me!"

Last winter, I spent a very cold and dark night at the battlefield pavilion off East Elm with two members of Outkazt Paranormal and my twenty-one-year-old niece Jade. Using the spirit box, we asked several questions. Most responses from the spirit box were unintelligible, but the one that I will recall for the rest of my life is after we asked if "they" knew our names. Out of the speaker, loud and forcefully, came a male voice: "JAAADE." Right afterward, you can hear us on the multiple audio and video recorders yell

Left: River Raisin National Battlefield Park. The East Elm Avenue entrance to the pavilion, battle history signs and park trails. *Photo by Samuel D. Holland.*

Below: The interior of the former River Raisin Battlefield Museum. *Photo by Jeri Holland, 2019.*

in glee. We didn't even hear what "they" said right afterward. On an active night, the atmosphere is palpable.

The feelings you embody on the battlefield are truly unique and familiar at the same time. It's not always a feeling of being watched but the feeling of activity all around you, playing like a movie and you just stepped in the center of it, and everyone ignores you and carries on. And I find that the more you go, the more experiences you have.

As one of the area's bloodiest conflicts, the War of 1812 has yielded a great number of ghostly sightings here. Do places where violent deaths occur somehow absorb the horror, only to conjure up images that haunt the living for generations to come?

If you're interested in the Battle of Frenchtown and the subsequent massacre, you can visit 1403 East Elm Avenue for the small parking lot and the trail through the battlefield. The new River Raisin National Battlefield Visitors Center is at 333 North Dixie Highway.

Embrace the history and "Remember the Raisin!"

CHAPTER 6

THE BLOODY TELEGRAPH

A KILLER ROAD

Originally a telegraph maintenance path, today's Telegraph Road is a stretch of U.S. 24, one of the main thoroughfares through southeastern Michigan. Since Telegraph Road was created in the mid-nineteenth century, it's been the site of countless deaths. An inherently deadly stretch of road, busy Telegraph Road has become infamous for the lives it has claimed. The death toll has been so high that the highway has ultimately earned itself a macabre nickname: "The Bloody Telegraph."

In 1848, the president of the Erie and Michigan Telegraph Company, John James Speed, ordered the first telegraph lines installed between Detroit and Toledo for use on the adjacent Michigan Central Railroad. As the lines were installed, a path was needed to provide access for maintenance of the telegraph poles. So was born a small dirt road along the telegraph line. Despite the road's official purpose, local horse-drawn wagons and carriages utilized it as well.

As automobiles became more commonplace with the turn of the twentieth century, the old dirt road was improved for greater traffic. In 1919, Telegraph Road became designated as U.S. 10. It soon became a major road running south from Detroit, the automobile manufacturing capital of the world.

The name of U.S. 10 was changed to U.S. 24 when the United States Numbered Highway System was inaugurated on November 11, 1926. It was then that Telegraph Road became an important arterial thoroughfare south of Detroit.

As the road's traffic increased, more accidents occurred and more and more lives were claimed. As any student of the supernatural knows, bloody accidents leave imprints on a roadway and become a paranormal gateway.

Telegraph Road's importance as a through route between Detroit and Toledo was diminished when I-75 opened in the late 1950s as the first interstate highway in the state, soon followed by I-94. By 1930, automobiles were reaching more dangerous speeds of fifty to sixty miles per hour. It was around this time that the *Battle Creek Enquirer* informed the public that U.S. 24 had been declared the worst stretch of highway in the state. The state counted twenty-one fatal accidents within Monroe County in 1931—an almost unheard-of number for a twenty-nine-mile stretch of road.

The state decided to invest in a million-dollar program that would widen the interstate roads within Michigan. Grover C. Dillman, state highway commissioner, declared that widening and straightening of U.S. 24 was a must for Monroe County. The work launched in 1932 and continued through 1938. It was during this time that "the Phantom Bridge," built in the 1920s, was abandoned for a wider, smoother route over Stony Creek. More about the Phantom Bridge later.

Sixty-nine traffic deaths occurred on Telegraph Road within Monroe County in 1936. Forty-six persons were killed in 1937. In 1938, forty-eight persons lost their lives in car accidents. On February 15, 1939, the state implemented a speed limit of fifty miles per hour on the stretch of road

Telegraph Road and Stony Creek Road. The Phantom Bridge is at the top and center. You can see where the road once existed before it was widened and straightened. *Courtesy of Google Maps.*

Telegraph Road and West Hurd Road. Here, too, you can see where the road once was prior to the 1930s. *Courtesy of Google Maps.*

from the Ohio state border through Monroe County. Within six months, the death rate for the Monroe County section of U.S. 24 had declined by 68 percent. But it was to be short-lived—no pun intended.

In 1955, a headline from the front page of the *Detroit Free Press* blared "Killer Telegraph Road Takes Record Toll!" The secondary heading was no better: "Bloody US-24, Michigan's most dangerous highway, is racking up a ghastly new slaughter record." It's enough to send chills down your spine. U.S. 24 had become a "death-a-mile highway." Accidents were wiping out entire families. Causes ranged from head-on-collisions to speeding to wintry weather causing vehicles to spin out of control.

An article in the 1955 edition of the *Holland Evening Sentinel* reported, "1954 had 57 traffic deaths, 22 just on Telegraph Road through Monroe County."

In 1964, the Detroit-Toledo Expressway and the new U.S. 23 Expressway were constructed. These roads were expected to reduce traffic fatalities and to take some of the traffic burden off Telegraph Road. That year, Telegraph Road in Monroe County had only four fatalities.

It seemed the new expressways worked. Again—only for a time.

Even though the deaths numbered in the thousands over the last century, some deaths stood out more than others in the local newspaper archives. For example, two separate drivers were charged with negligent homicide in a bus-versus-truck accident on Telegraph Road in May 1929. Five persons were killed and sixteen injured in one accident alone. Both drivers pleaded not guilty.

Deaths on the Bloody Telegraph haven't just been car-versus-car accidents.

Pedestrian Leroy Boughton, fifty-five years old, of LaSalle Township, was killed on the evening of December 27, 1935. He had been walking along the highway just seven miles south of the city of Monroe.

In March 1935, another pedestrian, fifty-one-year-old LaSalle steelworker Ed Larrow, was also mowed down by a motorist. Tragically, the accident left a literal trail of blood along old Telegraph Road. Not long after the pedestrian was hit, a Toledo driver stopped at a filling station at the intersection of Telegraph and West Erie Roads and reported to the attendant that they had followed a car for about five miles; it had been carrying the body of a man on its running board. The car had a Michigan license plate with a University of Michigan permit tag, the witness reported. The gas station operator relayed the information, along with a few of the tag's numbers obtained by the witness, to the Monroe deputies. Law enforcement began the grisly search for the body along Telegraph Road. The body was found early the next morning by Elton Elliot, lying in the middle of the highway just in front of his home.

Less than twenty-four hours later, law enforcement had located the driver, twenty-seven-year-old Charles Rorabacher, of Ann Arbor. The automobile was found about five miles away, hidden in a garage with front-end damage. Rorabacher was given a $1,000 bond and bound over for trial in the circuit court on charges of negligent homicide. He was sentenced to one to five years in the Michigan reformatory at Ionia after pleading guilty of leaving the scene of an accident. Ed Larrow was survived by a wife and seven children.

The very day Larrow's body was found, another two men—ages nineteen and thirty-three—were killed in a head-on collision between a car and truck on the same stretch of Telegraph Road.

At the writing of this chapter, the most recent pedestrian-versus-vehicle accident was in February 2023. A woman was killed by a southbound car while crossing Telegraph Road at the Kimberly Estates intersection. The woman was pronounced dead at the scene by medical personnel.

Now, if you've ever done your share of ghost hunting, you'll guess that this dark, bloody passageway through Monroe County would potentially house a smorgasbord of ghosts. And you'd be right.

When I requested any strange sightings or experiences, I received a slew of stories, both from Ohio residents who've traveled northward and from residents in eastern Michigan. The reports didn't seem to be of regular run-of-the-mill ghosts, either.

There's talk of lost souls wandering around asking if they're dead, apparitions of terrifying scenes replaying on the side of the road and spirits that like to give drivers a scare once in a while by popping up in the middle of the road—just briefly enough to make the motorists think they've hit a pedestrian.

Many people have lost power in electronics while traveling through this dead zone. Several people have reported their favorite playlist on Spotify has gone haywire and scrambled their music to unintelligible words. Occasionally, car lights, inside and out, have gone off for about two seconds before flashing back on again. Two seconds doesn't seem long—but when you're driving fifty miles per hour, it feels like a super long ten minutes.

Drivers on Telegraph Road have been said to encounter unexplainable sightings—for instance, some have reported seeing people walking along the berm of the road, but as they got closer, there was no one really there. Spooky, right? Sometimes, like in another chapter in this book, there are accounts of drivers pulling over to help someone on the side of the road, but once stopped they find not a soul around. Well, maybe a soul—but no living person.

Left: This roadway was once Telegraph Road before it was rerouted in the 1930s. *Photo by Samuel Holland*.

Right: Stony Creek. I'm unsure why the nearby road is called Stoney Creek and the actual creek is spelled Stony. *Photo by Samuel Holland*.

The Phantom Bridge that crosses over Stoney Creek. *Photo by Samuel Holland.*

Earlier, I briefly mentioned the fifty-foot Phantom Bridge. The structure was abandoned in the mid-1930s when the state widened and straightened Telegraph Road; it sits near the intersection of Telegraph and Stoney Creek Roads. People have spotted small lights floating in this area. At times they have been reported as red, other times white. There have been more than two occasions when explorers have heard a child call out to his daddy. Could this be one of the many children who have died along Telegraph Road? Is one still searching for his dad after being thrown from a car? Who knows at this point. Perhaps going out with dowsing rods and audio recorders may help us narrow down the details.

I can't say I've experienced anything myself at the Phantom Bridge or on Telegraph Road. But then again, I try to avoid the area as much as possible and take South Dixie Highway.

CHAPTER 7

THE VIVIAN ROAD FARMHOUSE

The Vivian Road farmhouse isn't the setting of *Amityville Horror*, *Poltergeist* or *The Haunting in Connecticut*, but it certainly could be. The old brick home sits on almost one and a half acres of land in Frenchtown Township. It was built in 1968, which goes to show that homes don't have to be centuries old to be haunted by poltergeists and ghosts. The home currently has three designated bedrooms and two bathrooms. There are also an office and a library that can each be converted to bedrooms, making five bedrooms in total.

Over the years, many of the home's inhabitants have reported experiencing unusual phenomena while in the home. According to the 2009 Halloween edition of the *Toledo Blade*, the Richards family—who lived in the house from 1979 to 1987—were one such family to report these experiences. Arthur, the Richardses' son, recalls several unusual occurrences within the Vivian Road house as a child.

Arthur's first spooky experience within the home took place one night when he was twelve years old. While in bed, he awoke to see his bedroom door slightly opened. He then saw a large dark shape enter his room and move over toward the bed. Arthur felt the bed shift as the visitor sat on the bed. Thinking the person was his stepdad, Arthur said, "Dad? What's going on, Dad? Something wrong?" No response. He reached over and turned his bedside light on—only to find no one in his room. Additionally, Arthur remembers several times hearing unexplained screams coming from the basement. The sounds made his hair stand on end.

Arthur wasn't the only member of his family to have hair-raising experiences while living in the home. Arthur's stepdad recalls that several times when he was in the shower, the musical potty chair in the corner of the bathroom would spontaneously start to play music.

Barry Brickey, Arthur's close childhood buddy, would often come to visit and for sleepovers. He witnessed lights turning off, doors mysteriously opening and closing and unexplained noises—noises that frightened him enough to send him fleeing from the house.

Barry remembers one such day on a very hot August afternoon in the 1980s when he was dropped off at his best friend's house. The teenager entered the front door and called out a greeting but received no response. He then heard footsteps upstairs, coming from his friend's bedroom. He ran upstairs, only to find Arthur's room empty. Being very familiar with the house, Barry checked the other upstairs rooms, but he still didn't find anyone home. He ran downstairs to use the phone at the bottom of the stairs to call a neighbor friend. As Barry stood at the bottom of the stairs placing the call, he felt a sudden rush of frigid air. While the phone rang, he heard thick, heavy footsteps coming downstairs. Barry sprouted goosebumps and subsequently freaked out when he next heard a door slam shut upstairs. He banged the phone down on its base and immediately ran outside. Terrified, he sat on a boulder on the side of the driveway to wait. About five minutes later, Arthur and his family pulled into the drive.

After explaining his experience, Arthur's parents shared with Barry that they would hear the dryer and television turning on and off spontaneously. There were other incidents that made Arthur's mother not want to be alone in the home, she said. She claimed hands and fingers would violate her in the dead of night. Arthur's stepdad then shared a story about when he was sleeping in the master bedroom and was bitten on the side by something he assumed was demonic.

Barry recounted yet another time when he witnessed the family van stop running while in the driveway. It wouldn't restart, but once it was pushed out into the road, the van started and ran perfectly fine.

Everyone in the neighborhood knew about this house back in the 1980s. The boys' friends would all come over to check out the house. One high school boy, frightened out of his wits, ended up calling his dad to pick him up from a party that the teens were having. His truck, too, had stopped running while in the driveway. The boys decided to try what had worked in the past: they rolled the truck out of the driveway. It worked.

After Barry became an adult, he wrote a book called *The Silence*, based loosely on the Vivian Road house. Sometime later, he was invited back to the home for an investigation by the current renters. He recently relayed his experience to me:

> *I ran up the ladder to the attic and sat on the landing, then I took pictures below me facing the second floor and then around the attic. As I was going up into the attic, a male's voice shouted from behind me, "Hey!" I turned around, [but I] was alone. It was dark, but the moon was illuminating enough to see. I noticed that there was a lightbulb and drawstring above my head on the ceiling. It was hot, with no wind. After I took some pictures, I looked back up at that lightbulb string, and it was swinging back and forth. It was very creepy!*

Barry was asked to go down to the basement with the woman leading the investigation of the house:

> *They weren't getting many responses, so she brought me down to communicate with a possible spirit, as I had a history with the house. I was holding dowsing rods while we asked questions, and we got immediate direct responses from a young child. The dryer came on a couple of times. It was a newer dryer and [had] no issues with wiring. The push start button was perfect height for a small child, too. This is something that the two previous renters mentioned about hearing. While I was asking questions to the child, I felt fingers rake across my back, which were cold and freaked me out! I asked if they did that to me, and the rods immediately moved. I'm usually very skeptical about things like that, or try to make sense of it, but I tried not to move the rods, but sure enough, they moved on their own to direct questions. The woman who I was with was also recording everything. The recorder was right behind me. She suddenly stopped and went over to the device, and the battery was drained and dead!*

Many of the Vivian Road renters during the 1990s reported more of the same. One of the previous renters recalled that her baby monitor often produced the sound of her baby crying, but when she checked on her child, the baby was sleeping. Others reported a spirit closing and opening cupboards, doors and drawers. Lights continued to go off and on even after the owner had an electrician check the house. Haunting footsteps stepped solidly from the second floor, attic and staircases. A black shadow reportedly lurked around the house.

In the 2010s, Randy and Hollie Gray moved into the house with their two young sons, unaware of the spooky—and sometimes terrifying—occurrences that were known to take place in the home. Hollie shared their experiences with me:

My husband has always worked midnights, so most evenings I was alone with the boys. The first thing that started to freak me out was the "voices." The boys had bedrooms upstairs, and once it got dark, after [putting] them to bed, I would hear one of them yelling "Mom! Mom!" I would run up the stairs only to find them both soundly sleeping. At first, I thought I was just hearing things, but the frequency grew, and it began to happen almost every night. I had a friend over one night, and she got to hear it for herself. It scared her to the point that she wouldn't come back into the house—ever. We regularly heard footsteps and voices when no one else was around. Large pockets of cold air would pass through the room almost like a breeze but with no wind.

I have collected porcelain dolls since I was a young girl. When my grandmother passed away, I was given one of her dolls. She is made of solid porcelain, and she is about two feet tall. I kept her on a stand in a glass curio cabinet. One day we got up and my stepdaughter noticed that both of the doll's eyes were missing. I had the worst feeling wash over me when I looked at it. Felt like pure dread and made me feel physically ill.

The absolute worst thing that we experienced happened to my husband. He was a strong skeptic and usually blew off the weirdness, but I have never seen him more frightened. We were using the room off the main living room on the first floor as our bedroom; the other bedrooms were all upstairs. One afternoon when Randy was sleeping (he slept in the day because he worked at night), he ran from the bedroom sweaty, pale and gasping for air. He was scared like I have never seen him. He said he was woken by something sitting on his chest. The room was pitch black, but he felt the weight of it on his chest, and when he opened his eyes, he could make out its wings and feel its breath on his face. He was completely frozen in terror. He literally immediately ripped our bed out of that room and refused to ever sleep in it again. We basically kind of shut the door and avoided it as much as possible.

Things continued on for the Gray family. One evening, Hollie was picking up around the living room before heading to bed. She carried some dishes into the kitchen, and when she reentered the living room, the drawer on the end table was wide open. Other times the television would go on and off, doors would open and close and lots of other small things would occur that the family just got used to. The Grays ended up living in the house for about six years until one afternoon the attic mysteriously caught fire. The house was damaged but not destroyed. Afterward, the house sat empty until November 2022, when the nonresidential owner finally sold the vacant house.

Why is this house haunted?

The area along present-day Vivian Road and beyond was originally settled by Native Americans, specifically the Potawatomi, hundreds of years before French settlers reached the forest-covered area in the late 1600s. Local Indians had trading relations with French Canadians at that time. In fact, Barry Brickey has said the area contained Native American artifacts, and some were even found when digging in the home's garden.

Forests eventually gave way to farmland in the area where the house sits, before the Vivian Road house was ultimately built in 1968. Fifteen years later, Arthur's mom did some research, finding that three people had died within the house just a few short years after it was built.

I won't reveal the farmhouse's exact address, but you can check out Barry K. Brickey's book *The Silence*, which originally stemmed from the home. The book can be purchased through Amazon and local bookstores.

CHAPTER 8

OLD MILL MUSEUM

O n the banks of the River Raisin, in present-day Dundee, Michigan, sits an old, historic mill. The history of Dundee's Old Mill is rich, arguably some of the richest history in all of Michigan. The site is listed in the National Register of Historic Places, and the mill itself has been converted to a museum.

Prior to the late 1700s, the Potawatomi tribe and other bands of Indigenous peoples inhabited the land in and around the village of Dundee, where the mill would ultimately come to be. By 1796, as part of northwestward expansion, the United States had begun occupying lands in southeast Michigan, pushing Native Americans off their land. As of the 1820s, Dundee and the surrounding region had begun to be settled by white people. The village itself was incorporated in 1855.

William Remington first purchased the plot on July 23, 1823. In 1828, the first sawmill was built there by Riley Ingersoll, along with Samuel and William Gale. The very first dam was made from brush and dirt and was simultaneously built to power the mill.

According to the *Democratic Free Press*, Sybrant Van Nest turned the mill into grist in 1832. In 1846, the dam was redone with logs, a sturdier material. Soon after, in 1848, the original mill was torn down and a new three-story frame gristmill was built by Dundee pioneer Alfred Wilkerson.

In 1880, Wilkerson sold the mill to Henry Smith of Berlin Township for $8,000. Two years later, it changed hands yet again when Ramus Brouwer

Dundee's Old Mill Museum. *Photo by Jeri Holland, 2020.*

Davis purchased the mill. Davis built a new rafter dam in 1897, using recycled timbers from an upstream railroad bridge that had fallen into disuse.

In 1910, Davis sold the lot to the Dundee Hydraulic Power Company, which built a concrete dam on the site. Next, C.W. Ward purchased both the mill and the dam. Immediately after acquiring the site, he erected a new dam, twenty-two inches higher than the previous one. He intended to manufacture electric power. The new dam, however, caused a lot of trouble, as it flooded a wide surrounding berth of farmland, which naturally perturbed numerous farmers. Ward was subsequently required to lower the dam to its previous height.

In the 1920s, Detroit Edison acquired the rights to power the village of Dundee. Shortly thereafter, the old mill was purchased by George Voorhees, but the mill stood abandoned until the 1930s. By 1931, village officials had voted to demolish the building. All was not lost, however. A new owner stepped forward—an owner who would, before long, become world renowned. Henry Ford informed the village of Dundee that he had big plans for the substantially sized mill on the River Raisin.

From 1932 to 1935, Ford kept approximately sixty men working at the mill. He stripped the building to its original timber frame and essentially

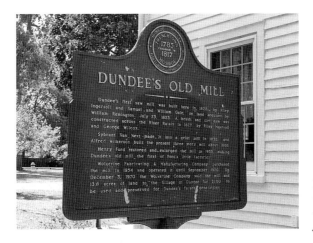

Dundee historical marker that sits outside the main entrance to the mill. *Photo by Jeri Holland.*

rebuilt it from the ground up. Henry Ford also installed new generators, a foundry and steam boilers. His new factory was now part of his grand design for dotting the countryside with village industries. According to an article in the 1935 *Detroit Free Press*, several young men from Dundee were asked by Henry Ford interests to come to Dearborn. From there, they were instructed in the operation of machinery to be installed in the "Old Davis grist mill." Automobile parts would be manufactured in the old mill, operated by water power from the river.

Ford's Dundee plant ultimately produced welding tips for Ford's main automobile factories. In the Depression era, the plant was of major importance to the local economy. Prior to Ford's acquisition of the Old Mill, Dundee was a sleepy old town, by all accounts past its prime and on the decline. The place seemed destined to be all-but-forgotten by 1935, when Henry Ford, who loved small towns, began setting up the mill with state-of-the-art equipment for casting and machining hard copper. The finished parts were destined for use in Ford's plants, mostly for electrodes used in welding. The welding electrodes were then shipped from Dundee to Ford's plants throughout the world.

Eventually, the new Ford plant was providing great employment for eighty men in and around Dundee. A classroom was arranged on-site to teach the new employees blueprint reading and shop mathematics, two subjects necessary for the work. Their daily pay was a whopping $8—equivalent to $170 today.

The newly renovated mill, fresh dam and—most importantly—new jobs transformed the town. Tumbling-down houses were rebuilt or repaired, new stores were constructed and there wasn't a single able-bodied man

Ford Mill reconstruction in 1935. *Courtesy of Old Mill Museum.*

within the village limits on public relief throughout the Depression and subsequent war.

In 1938, Mayor Frank Wilcox told the *Detroit Free Press*, "The plant is the best thing that ever happened to this town. Our relief problem disappeared as soon as the plant got going, and all lines of business perked up. I guess nobody is getting rich, but everybody lives pretty comfortably."

After Henry Ford's death in 1947, the mill gradually declined, and the plant was ultimately sold to Wolverine Manufacturing Company in 1954. The company converted the plant into a paper mill to produce gasket material. In 1970, Wolverine sold the landmark to the Village of Dundee for one dollar.

As in the old adage, history is bound to repeat itself—the mill stood unused for the next decade until 1981, when the Old Mill Restoration Committee, a group of community volunteers, undertook the daunting mission of turning the mill structure into a museum.

The Restoration Committee accomplished their goal; the Old Mill Museum is now often referred to as the oldest and most notable museum in Michigan. Three floors of the historic mill showcase Dundee's local history—from the time when the Potawatomi Indians inhabited the land to life in the Victorian-era village and, of course, the automobile industry.

Today, the haunted Old Mill Museum offers visitors a perfectly creepy look into the mill's operations and exposes the spookier side of its long history. Paranormal researchers and mill employees alike have picked up heaps of bizarre happenings. In fact, the Old Mill Museum is so haunted that it boasts its own in-house paranormal group called Spirit World Paranormal Investigations (SWPI), a group based out of southeast Michigan with members from both Ohio and Michigan.

SWPI has been the volunteer host of afterhours public and private ghost hunts at the Old Mill Museum since October 2011. They also hold the Old Mill ParaFest, an annual paranormal convention and ghost hunt. The convention hosts a variety of speakers, from television personalities to paranormal specialists, authors and ghost-hunting groups from all over. These events and investigations help the Old Mill Museum raise money to sustain itself financially.

Adam Wcislek of SWPI told me the tours aren't for the faint of heart. "Once they [visitors] have their first experience here, it's so profound, they actually end up running out of the mill," Wcislek said.

"We were in the banquet hall [within the museum], and we were making sure it was all straightened up, doors closed," Wcislek recalled. "A volunteer says, 'I dare you to move a table,' and all of a sudden, the table slid two or three feet. We were all a little startled at that point."

Nancy, an Old Mill Museum tour guide, had a small but significant interaction back in 2009. "The one day I really remember, when I knew something was happening, I was getting ready to leave and I was going up these stairs to turn off the lights and I heard the bell on the door ring," she said.

I interviewed Tim Rehahn, organizer of ParaFest and the liaison between SWPI and the Old Mill Museum. I first asked him if any experiences at the Old Mill Museum stood out in his mind. His response was as follows:

We had our first investigation there in 2011, before the Old Mill Museum considered having public investigations. As we were getting set up, Tim D. and I were looking to see where we wanted the DVR and other cameras and equipment. We walked over by the bar and asked Donna and Jeanne, who was the psychic medium we worked with, where they think will be hot spots. Donna says, "I think we should have cameras here, by the bar." At that moment, a voice said, "One camera."

Back when we started volunteering to offer the public investigations, [there] *was a second group that came during November 2011. We gave the group a tour, and Tim D. and I were walking side by side. I was talking to him when I suddenly felt a couple taps on my shoulder, as if he wanted to get my attention. I looked over and said, "Yeah, Tim? Tim?" He wasn't there—nobody was. He was back by the bar; I was in the middle of the large hall. Nobody or nothing was near me.*

Again, while in the large hall, a group [of investigators] *were asking whoever they'd seen walking by the door in the storage room previously to turn on the light. The door was open, and the light was coming on by command. So, I had to go see. They counted to 3, said, "On 3, turn it on!" After a couple times, someone said, "Maybe it's just the timing? Let's count to 10." They counted "1, 2, 3, 4, 5, 6, 7, 9," BOOM, light comes on. Kind of cool. We told* [fellow SWPI ghost hunter] *Rich when he came into the room. We said, "Can you show Rich that you can turn it on?" The light came on!*

A few years back, I was setting the cameras up in the large hall when Rich walked in the door. The camera picked up on someone saying, "Hey man" as Rich walked by. I thought someone must have been messing with me, so I checked another camera angle that showed nobody was around except Rich, and he wasn't talking.

One day, we had a group investigating. I decided to take a walk around to check and make sure everything was going okay. I went to the large hall and thought, "I'm going to sit down." At the time, the cubby in the back left didn't have the doors; it was open and set up like a living room for pictures, etc. I sat down on the couch and kicked my feet up. About five minutes later, I hear footsteps, like someone from the group was walking up. To avoid frightening anyone, I said, "I'm in here on the couch." There was no reply, but the walking got louder, closer. A shadow figure wearing a cowboy hat walked over, sat at the table in front of the opening to the cubby in front of me. He sat with his back to me, and you could see him stretch his arm out, lift it up as if he was taking a drink. When it went back, you could hear a glass hit the table as if he was drinking. He finished his drink, got up and walked away. I only had a camera on me, but nothing showed up. No evidence but great experience.

I followed up with another question that had piqued my interest—does a little girl really haunt the basement?

I know many teams have seen a little girl in the basement. Adam says it looks like Nevaeh. She was first seen in the office; our director Shirley said her dog wouldn't go in there. She brought him with her many times to the mill, but he wouldn't go in the office, he was scared. Since it's off limits to the public, she wanted a couple from our group to check it out. Adam and I believe Andy went in there. Since I wasn't there, I don't know all the details, but they saw or heard something under the desk, and Adam said it was a little girl. He started talking to him (he's a psychic medium), and when he came out of the office, he described her. I immediately got goosebumps and said, "That sounds like Nevaeh." I helped out by searching for her when she went missing. I volunteered a couple times to search. I pulled up a picture online, and as soon as he saw the picture, he said, "That's her!"

In 2009, five-year-old Nevaeh Buchannon was abducted while playing outside her Monroe apartment. The only sign left behind was the scooter the little girl was known to use to zoom around her apartment complex. On June 4, eleven days after Nevaeh went missing, her small body was found on the banks of the River Raisin, just off Dixon Road near the Old Mill Museum. Two persons of interest were identified during the early investigation—both men were convicted sex offenders—but neither was charged. Her murder remains unsolved. A weathered memorial now sits on the side of Dixon Road, a few hundred feet from where the body was found. There's a tall cross, flowers and permanent landscaping with several stones that adorn Nevaeh's name—*Heaven* spelled backward.

I next asked Tim if he recalled any other ghosts and asked what sort of things he had experienced at the mill over the years. He responded:

Milton is in the men's bathroom and Henrietta in the women's bathroom in the large hall.

It's not uncommon for me to see shadow figures, or people walking/talking all over the building. In fact, here's a great experience. One time just before COVID-19, I was coming in through the [Marjorie E. Busz Conference Room] *Busz Room door; we were getting ready to host a group. I was early, and when I opened the door and walked in, I saw a man in a suit and hat in the generator room. He looked over, smiled, tipped his hat and turned around, walking into the archive room. I walked over that way to see who it was. There was nobody in there, [so I] walked into the archive room, and nobody was there. Then it suddenly dawned on me—I think it was Henry Ford! I looked at a picture [of him], and it sure was!*

Another quick thing I remember: a group came in to investigate, and using an Ovilus in the pantry, they were asking questions and getting answers. One asked, "Can you see into the future?" It said, "Yes." So he asks, "Who is going to win the [presidential] election?" At the time, Mitt Romney and Barack Obama were running. The Ovilus said, "Obama." The guy says, "Oh great, another four years of Obama?" Then the Ovilus says, "Assassinate." I told him I wouldn't put that online; we didn't want the audio or stories out there, because if President Obama did happen to have something happen, we didn't need any issues with the Secret Service, etc. Would be a bit tough to explain.

Other groups have joined SWPI on occasion. Back in 2012, Marter Paranormal Research Team and 313 Paranormal Society collaborated on a joint investigation. They experienced flashes of light, EMF reactions, mists and responsive EVPs. And that was just from the chamber room display.

The Great Lake Ghost Hunters of Michigan have reported obtaining responses from a spirit box during a session in the basement. The kitchen and dining room displays seem to be quite active getting spirit box responses, EMF responses, arm touches and EVPs. They have gotten several electronic voice phenomena, with the basement being the most popular. Some of the EVPs from the basement include "bitch," "chairs," "catch her," "coin face" and "don't do that." Some from the second floor include "call me," "get to work" and "it means everything."

Afterlife Road Productions explored the museum a couple times with SWPI and other paranormal investigators. They utilized audio recorders, video cameras, EMF detectors, spirit boxes (they were called Franks boxes in my day) and thermal cameras. The group experienced high EMF (electromagnetic field) spikes throughout the building while collecting EVPs. They routinely heard footsteps on the third floor while on the second floor. They heard voices that were both picked up on recorders and one or two that weren't.

One experience seemed to shake a man to his core. A museum barrier rope unhooked nearby and ricocheted back to its pole, then tipped over. Even a seasoned ghost hunter can scream bloody murder, apparently. The group went back to the same area and tried to get a repeat experience—spiritually and man-made. They were not able to replicate the movements. Instead, they tried to get a paranormal repeat response, but that, too, was a no-go.

The group also tried to do solo investigations in the basement. It didn't last too long before strange knocks and footsteps were heard and tangible items moved across the floor. Running away was the first response of the

Dundee's Old Mill Museum chamber display. *Photo by Jeri Holland, 2020.*

investigators, but they soon returned to unsuccessfully debunk the experience. All were in good spirits at the end of the investigation.

While no deaths are known to have occurred inside the Old Mill, there are documented deaths at the dam and rumored deaths on the property itself. Documented drownings are that of an eighteen-year-old named Joseph in 1912, a nineteen-year-old named Leon in 1930 and a five-year-old girl who drowned at the park while on a picnic near the mill in 1960.

There are four main reasons the Old Mill Museum in Dundee is believed to be haunted. First, much of the mill was built from limestone, first taken from under the dam next to the museum. Limestone can "save" energies just like an old-fashioned VCR or cassette tape. Next, spirits need energy to show themselves, whether through EVP, EMF, apparition and so on. The museum created power for much of the last 150-plus years. In fact, the mill still houses the old generator. Thirdly, it has been said that water—or running water to be more exact—tends to increase energy and activity. The historic mill has an abundance of running water; the River Raisin is right outside the doors. Finally, antiques are also believed to hold specters, and the museum has three floors full of them.

Little girl clothing display at Old Mill Museum in Dundee. *Photo by Jeri Holland, 2020.*

I first visited the Old Mill Museum in September 2020, during the first year of the pandemic, at a time when I very much needed a break away from the house. I had heard talk that the mill was haunted, but otherwise, I went in not knowing anything. As a history lover, I was enamored by the three floors of what must have been hundreds of displays. As a deep-down ghost hunter, I felt pulled to the little girls' clothing displayed on the third floor. The other area that piqued my interest was the kitchen and dining area. I did not record because there was another couple in the building and a museum employee (all maintaining distance from each other), and I didn't want to risk contamination.

After speaking to SWPI and doing the research for this chapter, I can't wait to go back for a full-fledged investigation.

The website for Spirit World Paranormal Investigations is www. michiganghost.com.

CHAPTER 9

LAKE MONROE

A n abandoned old quarry of hair-raising lore, Lake Monroe lies off Laplaisance Road in Monroe County. Legend has it that ghosts of long-dead souls haunt the inky depths of the lake, just waiting to snatch their next victim in retaliation. For nearly a century, tales of suspicious drownings and disappearances in and around the quarry have run rampant among locals. Among young people who have dared to swim to the depths of the lake, stories abound of mysterious underwater sightings. Before the quarry filled completely, others reported seeing shadowy figures dive from the rocky cliffs that ensconce the lake—only to never hear a splash. And others still have simply disappeared, seemingly taking their harrowing tales with them.

In early 1907, Grassly & Guttman purchased a plot of land off Laplaisance Road for the purpose of creating a stone quarry in Monroe. At the time, there were already two other lucrative quarries in the area, so the men were confident the quarry had the makings of a prominent business. Long-term success for the men, however, was not to be. In 1911, the quarry was put up for sale. It was purchased by France Stone Company and then fell into disuse. The land eventually became privately owned. Once barren, the one-hundred-foot-deep quarry began to fill with groundwater. By the late 1990s, the quarry had become the lake it is today. Thus, France Stone Quarry became Lake Monroe.

Immediately after it was abandoned and began to fill, the quarry became a hotspot for local swimmers. Since those early days, seemingly endless accidents and deaths have occurred here. Despite clear signage warning would-be swimmers to stay away and the threat from the Monroe County sheriff that trespassers would risk being issued citations and having their vehicles towed, unlawful visitors have continued to find any way they can to access the property.

One of the earliest deaths attributed to the stone quarry was that of Phillip Patsie in 1916. Patsie, age forty at the time, was employed at the France Stone Quarry, where his job involved loading stone into mining cars. As the story goes, one day a loaded car lost control and began to roll unhindered down toward Patsie. Coworkers tried to warn him, but their shouts could not be heard above the noise of the quarry. Unaware of the imminent danger, Patsie remained directly in the path of the runaway vehicle and was killed instantly when it ran him over. He left behind three children and a wife.

A similar accident happened in April 1928 when a twenty-four-year-old Italian laborer named Albert Fabitt sustained serious internal injuries after being run over by a quarry locomotive attached to a car in the quarry pit.

Could these accidents and others have contributed to the subsequent hauntings?

By the 1930s, the first reports of strange sounds emanating from the quarry had begun to circulate among local gossip. Although the quarry was already abandoned, it was said that dynamite blasts and movement of stone mining cars on their tracks could be heard bouncing off the stone walls. As the years went on, reports of sounds only increased.

In July 1941, tragedy again struck at the quarry when nine-year-old Margaret Rosonski fell from the rocky edge into the water. Little Margaret had walked with a playmate from her house on Conant Avenue to explore the old quarry. She drowned before the friend could find help. Her family had her buried at Saint Joseph Cemetery.

In 1944, another life was taken when a local eleven-year-old boy named Glen drowned in a cut in the quarry. Thirty-five years later, tragedy at the quarry struck the family again when Glen's nephew—his brother's then thirteen-year-old son, Brian—was found dead in a shallow section of the quarry, directly under a 120-foot ledge. The boy's father was quoted as saying his son had last been seen about 11:30 a.m. the day before at his school, about half a mile from the quarry. Monroe County sheriff's deputies announced at the time that Brian had probably fallen to his death after accessing the property of the unfenced quarry. His body was discovered by local searchers. Brian's heartbroken father said to Monroe AP News, "This is the second life I've lost in that quarry. My brother drowned here when I was 6 years old, now my son...."

He went on to plead for more safety precautions to prevent any more tragedies. "There's quite a large, deep drop but only one short fence along the road. All the deaths and accidents that have happened at the quarry could have been prevented if there was a fence surrounding [the quarry]. How many more people will have to die before they do that?"

His efforts did not result in better fencing. Today, the same short fence is along the road, although large rocks have been placed on-site to block cars from driving through the property. However, children, teens and adults still find their way in.

In the early 2000s, two more incidents frightened a handful of young adults and they began to avoid Lake Monroe. One group of witnesses allegedly saw a man jump from a rocky ledge, sailing downward with his arms out toward the water. They happened to be jumping in as well, but upon surfacing, they saw neither hide nor hair of the leaping swimmer. Spooked, the group left and spread the cautionary tale.

Another story that circulated around this time was of a teenage girl who was pushed into the water by an unknown pair of hands. After being helped from the water, she questioned each one of her friends, but one by one, they each swore it hadn't been them. The teens left the area quickly, glad to be escaping with their lives.

In June 2012, a twenty-year-old Pontiac man trespassed with friends and went swimming at the quarry. While about twenty-five feet offshore, he began to struggle. One of his swimming companions, a young female, later reported nearly drowning herself as she, too, had been pulled under. She managed to break free, but the young man disappeared below the surface. The Monroe County sheriff's office recovered his body the same night. There was no readily apparent reason for his drowning.

On a hot August day in 2015, a nineteen-year-old man died at the quarry while swimming with his friends. His companions spotted him going under, but as they tried to help, they reported feeling pulled under as well. One of the friends shared with Fox2 Detroit that nearly fifty people had grabbed goggles and jumped in the water to try to find their friend, to no avail.

In July 2018, yet another nineteen-year-old male died while swimming in the quarry. Monroe Township fire chief Larry Merkle told the *Monroe News* that the Monroe County sheriff's dive team recovered the teen's body from the lake the following day. It was deemed suspicious, and an investigation ensued. Ultimately, the investigation determined that the cold water may

Lake Monroe, 2020. *Photo by Jeri Holland.*

have caused the teen's muscles to cramp, taking him down and causing his drowning.

In October 2018, a scuba diver went to local police after he spotted sunken cars while diving in Lake Monroe. The Monroe County and Monroe Township officials, along with a dive team, a towing company and others, pulled a Chevrolet Impala from the water. The body of a male was found inside the sunken car. It had likely been under water for an extended period of time. Also found under water there was an SUV that had been reported stolen out of Monroe County. That second vehicle was also pulled from the quarry. There was no known connection between the two finds.

What has brought about these deaths and others like it? What has caused young people to report apparitions jumping from ledges? What mysterious force has been pulling swimmers under the water and causing them to drown?

In the nineteenth century, the idea that environmental factors like air and rock-laden land could store traces of human emotions or play scenes over and over again like an old-fashioned VCR was introduced by scholars as an attempt to provide natural place memory explanations for supernatural phenomena. A good example of such a place is Gettysburg, Pennsylvania. The battlefields of Gettysburg are a truly haunted ground of granite, limestone and a tragic past embedded within the atmosphere.

In 1837, mathematician, philosopher, inventor and mechanical engineer Charles Babbage published a work on natural theology called *The Ninth Bridgewater Treatise*. Babbage hypothesized that spoken words leave permanent impressions in the air, even though they become inaudible after time. He suggested that it is possible due to transfer of motion between particles.

Could Phillip Patsie or Albert Fabitt still be working around the quarry? Are the apparitions of swimmers just victims replaying their scenes before they died? Are those reports of people being pushed into the water just rabble-rousers still playing around? Whatever the case may be, it's best to let the spirits lie or you'll put your life at risk.

Police want to remind locals that this is not a public lake, and those who trespass could be charged. They also remind folks that the extreme depth and rockiness of the quarry make it particularly dangerous.

CHAPTER 10

WOODLAND CEMETERY

Monroe's Woodland Cemetery was established in 1810, making it one of Michigan's oldest cemeteries. This historic cemetery spans eleven acres, and the history within the burial ground is quite rich. It contains an old potters' field as well as graves of veterans who served in every major conflict from the Revolutionary War forward. Woodland also has the distinction of having been Monroe's first cemetery to accept African Americans. Additionally, American forces may have crossed through the cemetery as part of their retreat during the Battle of the River Raisin on January 22, 1813.

I would think a cemetery would be the last place ghosts and spirits would want to be, but I have been proven wrong before. The ghosts at Woodland seem to be attracted to the beautiful, sun-drenched plot of land that sits at 438 Jerome Street. Of course, the atmosphere at night is somewhat… different.

Throughout the years, there have been multiple reports of ghostly figures wandering the cemetery grounds after dusk, when the neighborhood is quiet and still. Some ghosts have been dressed in soldiers' uniforms; others have been reported as forms dressed in flapper dresses from the 1920s and '30s. Boys have been spotted playing tag or on their knees shooting marbles. When the witnesses would come closer, however, they'd realize the children were wearing knickers or short pants and waistcoat-type jackets. For those who ventured to step even closer, the boys reportedly disappeared before their eyes into thin air.

Woodland Cemetery near the entrance. *Photo by Jeri Holland, 2021.*

Beginning in 1910, the talk of the town was that Woodland Cemetery was haunted by a man with long white whiskers who had been appearing to unsuspecting visitors from behind trees and shrubbery. He most commonly appeared near the vicinity of Fourth Street. By the late summer of 1911, the Monroe Police Department had had enough. A police officer was dispatched to the scene to make a careful determination of the situation of the long-whiskered gentleman.

The shadows of the night were falling fast, and the trees in the vicinity of the cemetery were casting an impenetrable gloom as the officer started up the path. Before long, he encountered the strange whiskered man and gave chase. But when the mysterious form darted into the depths of the graveyard, the officer lost his nerve and turned back from the creepy blackness.

Cemetery superintendent Brayton alerted the police of continuing reported appearances. About a month later, an older couple was walking down Fourth Street one evening when they spotted the man. They recognized him—it was a harmless old man who'd owned a vineyard near the cemetery, a man known to be out around his property at night in order to chase away grape thieves.

Woodland Cemetery. *Photo by Jeri Holland.*

After a bit of research, I believe that the long-whiskered man was none other than Joseph Sterling Sr., who was born in 1818 and passed away on May 18, 1891. Sterling learned winemaking in Europe and then came to Monroe to establish a vineyard and wine company. In fact, he was the very first to do so in Michigan. In 1868, he started the Pointe aux Peaux Wine Company. He later expanded his vineyard and encouraged other local farmers to grow grapes.

Joseph Sterling Sr. may have passed his vineyards and winery down through his family tree, but he appears to have not given up his job of lookout for grape thieves.

THE CUSTER PLOT

Notably, a burial plot belonging to the families of Monroe residents George Armstrong Custer and his wife, Elizabeth Bacon Custer, can be found at Woodland Cemetery, although neither is actually buried there.

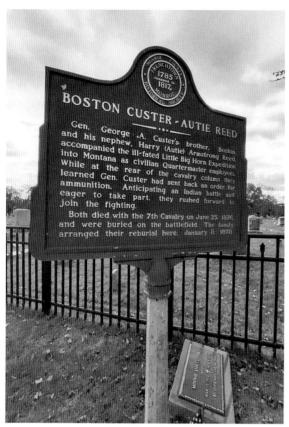

Left: The Boston Custer–Autie Reed historical sign. *Photo by Samuel D. Holland.*

Below: The Custer/Reed lot. *Photo by Samuel D. Holland.*

Upon approaching the plot, a historic plaque reads:

BOSTON CUSTER–AUTIE REED
General George A. Custer's brother, Boston, and his nephew Henry (Autie)
Armstrong Reed, accompanied the ill-fated Little Big Horn expedition into
Montana as civilian quartermaster employees. While at the rear of the
cavalry column they learned Gen. Custer had sent back an Indian battle
and eager to take part, they rushed forward to join the fighting. Both died
with the 7th Cavalry on June 25, 1876, and were buried on the battlefield.
Their family arranged their reburial here, January 8, 1878.

Boston and Henry Custer were reburied in Woodland Cemetery, but for some reason, the general was left behind. That is, his body was left behind. Custer's ghost, along with those of Boston and Henry, remains at the cemetery—in full uniform. While spirits typically show themselves in the quiet of the night, these ghostly soldiers have been known to appear in broad daylight, one in dark blue pants and the other two in light blue. Most have reported benign encounters with the burial ground's "residents." Several women, however, have claimed to have felt ghosts playing with their hair and derrières. Others have allegedly seen twenty-seven-year-old Boston Custer sitting in the trees, laughing.

The Woodland Cemetery is located at 438 Jerome Street, south of East Fourth Street, in the city of Monroe. The cemetery is open from 7:00 a.m. until 9:00 p.m.

CHAPTER 11

THE PAPERMILL

In 1910, construction of the River Raisin Paper Company mill began on the site of the River Raisin battlefield. The papermill remained operational until the 1980s, when the company went out of business. Fortunately, much of the property on which the factory once stood retained its archaeological integrity, and by the early 1990s, efforts were in progress to ensure the site was preserved for future generations. Later, two archaeological investigations found traces of a fence line behind which American troops fired from during the 1813 Battle of Frenchtown. Ultimately, the mill was torn down and the land was purchased by the city for use by the historical society. I can't help but wonder, given the strange happenings since it's closed, how many experiences the millworkers had while it was actually operational.

Twenty years ago, Tim Rehahn secured a job with Jeep at an overflow car lot in Monroe, near East Elm Avenue and North Dixie Highway. The lot was located behind the site where the old papermill had once stood. The aptly named Mill Road led to the Jeep overflow lot.

The papermill plant had shut its doors in 1995 after being operational for eighty-five years. The now-abandoned mill, owned by Homrich, Inc., sat on thirty acres of land on the site of a War of 1812 Frenchtown battle and the subsequent Frenchtown Massacre. (Covered in depth in an earlier chapter, the Frenchtown Massacre was a grisly affair in which an immense amount of terror and bloodshed was inflicted.)

Given the proximity of the overflow car lot to the horrific events of the Frenchtown Massacre—an event during which citizens and American soldiers were scalped, murdered and even burned alive—it's of little wonder that the security team of the Jeep car lot reportedly experienced several paranormal phenomena while on duty.

When Tim Rehahn first started working at the Monroe's Jeep overflow lot, he told me that not much happened. What did happen, the security team dismissed. Later, however, occurrences took place that they just couldn't explain.

In the corner next to the woods, behind the original battlefield museum, there was a generator light that just wouldn't cooperate. The light would shut off—they were the type of lights that once they're off, they had to cool down before they would go back on. So, for some time they'd be without light in that area. That particular light going off would happen frequently throughout the night—every night. The company that serviced the generator was called, but after checking the light, they said there wasn't a thing wrong with it. The issues, however, continued. The company was called again, at which time they decided to just replace it.

The fresh light did the same thing.

When the company came out a third time, they claimed the security team was overloading the generator by using it to charge their two-way radios. That sounded like a dodgy story, but the men moved their radios to another generator light. The first light continued to act up. With the fourth trip out, the company brought a brand-new generator light that they had previously run elsewhere for three days to make sure it worked. They installed the light at the Jeep lot.

That night it stopped working.

The light that they changed out was moved to another area of the lot, and it worked without any issues. At this time, there were murmurings that the lot and papermill were haunted, but they were dismissed.

Tim told me that one night, he was moving from post to post, filling in for other workers on break, assisting the supervisor, looking for trespassers. He left his station at the gate and drove by the faulty generator light. As he passed by, something hit his rear window with force. Tim immediately thought it was the supervisor playing a prank, but when he checked his mirrors, he saw no one. The supervisor was all the way at the other end of the parking lot.

A week or so later, Tim was assigned the job of opening the front gate and watching for trucks with auto transport trailers. Sitting in his security vehicle, he scanned the area continuously. Suddenly, he saw a man walk past the gate into the lot, directly in front of his driver side headlight. Tim opened his driver's side door and grabbed his radio. The intruder was wearing a blue-

and-white soldier's uniform. He stopped, looked at Tim, turned his head, took another step and disappeared. Tim sat in the truck reeling. He thought, "Did I really just see that?" He *was* working the night shift, and Tim knew he could easily get tired at night. Then again, he reminded himself, this was an old battlefield. Maybe…

Another night, Tim was stationed along the railroad tracks in the corner closest to the old papermill. His windows were down, and he was scanning the lot back and forth when all of a sudden something from the rear passenger side of his vehicle caught his attention. Tim did a double take. Less than twenty yards away, he saw a woman running—screaming as if she were being chased by a violent perpetrator. She ran over the tracks toward the Jeep lot. Tim grabbed his radio and opened the door to run to her. Then POOF! She was gone. No sound, no life. Nothing there. He tried again to talk down the eerie feeling creeping up inside. He stuck with his usual mantra: he was tired, and it had been a long shift.

One of the jobs of Tim and his co-workers was to catch people sneaking onto the papermill property and to call the police. Occasionally, the guards would see lights at the mill. One night, the lights inside the old building were quite active, so those on duty called the police. After checking the building, the police found no one. Later, the lights appeared once again. Not about to call the police for a second time, the security team watched. As soon as they'd see a light turn on, they'd pull out a spotlight and shine it into the building. Just before the morning hours, a lantern-like light floated around in a window of the decrepit papermill. Three of the security guards fired up their spotlights and blasted the window.

Nobody was inside. Not even a lantern.

A few weeks later, during the second shift, a black mass came tearing down the cement hill where a water tower sat. The mass continued toward the security vehicles at post number two. One of the security guards screamed at the sight of it. After it disappeared, she immediately asked if she could move to another post, but the supervisor denied her request. She quit, right then and there. The guard tore off the lot, throwing her radio out the window on her way out. A third-shift security guard also admitted he'd seen it one night; the "thing" had hit his car and put a dent into it. The guard said he was too frightened to move for a solid hour. Not long after that, the security team's supervisor was on the radio, razzing the guy. "You afraid the demons are going to get you?" he reportedly asked. As soon as he said "demons are going to get you," the radio changed to a voice that was a deep demonic sound. The rest of the transmission, before and after, was fine.

Finally, one winter night, Tim was manning post two when he spotted someone walking about halfway between posts two and three, quite a long distance to the other end of the lot. The person walked through the lot and into a row of Jeeps. Tim said he reported it to the supervisor on the radio. The supervisor and a coworker then searched but found no one. Afterward, the supervisor came around, parked and walked from post three toward Tim, asking him to show her exactly where he'd seen the person walking.

After checking one last time, she asked Tim, "You know what you have seen, right?"

"Yeah," he said, "a person walking on the lot. Maybe they hid well or ran when you guys headed that way."

"No," she said, "there's no footprints in the snow."

As they continued talking, Tim began thinking about all the strange things he'd witnessed over the past few months—the generator lights, the sightings and the strange calls on the two-way radios.

Tim had started the job at Jeep as a complete skeptic, but it finally dawned on him that enough was enough; there was absolutely no logical explanation for what he had experienced. Tim went on a quest to find a ghost hunter to check out the Jeep lot and the papermill grounds. He read everything he could and quickly learned that EVP stands for "electromagnetic voice phenomena." Within days, he had his first EVP. It wasn't long before Tim was a regular ghost hunter, and today, he is a team member of Spirit World Paranormal Investigations. He'll never forget what got him started: the ghosts of the River Raisin Battlefield.

CHAPTER 12

THE SAWYER HOMESTEAD

The beautiful old mansion sits at 320 East Front Street in the city of Monroe. It was listed as a historic site in 1975 and was listed in the National Register of Historic Places in 1977 for both its architectural and historical significance. The house is also part of the larger Old Village Historic District in Monroe.

The home, created in 1879 by Dr. Alfred I. Sawyer, sits on the original site of the François Navarre house, and according to the Monroe County Museum, there are several original timbers incorporated in the creation of the staircase banister.

François Navarre was the first permanent white settler in the present-day city of Monroe, Michigan. Twenty-year-old Navarre arrived in 1780 and began making friends with the Native Americans. They eventually gave him a deed for a five-hundred-acre farm along Nummasepee's (River Raisin) south bank on June 3, 1785. Almost one hundred settlers soon followed him there, building log cabins and living peacefully among the Indians for many years. Thus begun the town of Frenchtown, the precursor of Monroe. Navarre married Mary Suzor on November 9, 1790. Together they made a home in a log cabin on the property.

Navarre introduced a civil government and a court system there and is often called the "Father of Monroe." He was appointed a captain and then a colonel of the militia of the River Raisin. During the War of 1812, prior to the Battle of the River Raisin, he offered up his log cabin to General

Drawing of the François Navarre cabin that was built in 1785. *Postcard owned by Jeri Holland.*

James Winchester, who commanded American troops at the Battle of the River Raisin and used it as his headquarters before the battle began. In fact, he was staying overnight there when the battle broke out. Both Navarre and Winchester were captured nearby by the British. Navarre, in fact, was captured twice and managed to escape both times. When he returned to Frenchtown after the end of his service, he found it had suffered greatly during the war and its aftermath. He settled back in with his family on his farm in the little log cabin. Upon his death on September 1, 1826, his fourth son, Joseph Navarre, came home and took over running the farm.

After coming to Monroe, Dr. Alfred Isaac Sawyer and his wife, Sarah Toll, purchased and lived in the cabin from their marriage in 1859 until 1870. He then had the original log cabin demolished in 1873 and built the Italianate red brick home standing today. The two-story structure features fifteen rooms and a twelve-foot-square cupola.

Dr. Sawyer was one of the early advocates of homeopathic medicine. Even after an 1847 bill was introduced making it a jailable offense to practice homeopathy, he encouraged the University of Michigan to adopt the treatment. They ended up accepting it, but it took ten long years. He then served as president of the American Institute of Homeopathy Medicine and was witness to the first graduating class of the homeopathic department in 1877. According to his 1891 obituary in the *Detroit Free Press*, Dr. Sawyer was elected the mayor of Monroe in 1869, 1870 and 1877. He was also on the local school board for nine years.

The 1879 Sawyer Homestead was built by Dr. Alfred I. Sawyer. *Photo by Jeri Holland.*

The land the Sawyer Homestead sits on was home to the first white settler in Monroe County. *Photo by Jeri Holland.*

The home was given to the City of Monroe in 1938 by Jenny Toll Sawyer and has been used by a variety of organizations over the years, such as the Red Cross, Camp Fire Girls and Boy Scouts. In fact, the Sawyer Homestead also served as the first location for the Monroe County Historical Museum.

Once the last organization vacated the home, it stood empty until a group of citizens pooled their private funds and restored the building, creating an organization whose main reason for existence was the maintenance of the historic structure. Today, the Sawyer Homestead is mainly used for events and occasional displays.

Is the Sawyer Homestead haunted? I've been asking around for the past two years and have come across very few people who have investigated here. Those who have haven't gathered much evidence or even experienced anything paranormal. Heading there one afternoon, I encountered a friendly woman who worked there twice a week. She noticed I was checking out the building and taking photographs, and she introduced herself. She didn't offer many details but admitted they had issues with doors opening and closing, lights going off and on and the occasional footsteps when no one was in the home besides her. A few weeks later, I contacted the Homestead and the Board of Directors and got a "Yes, it's haunted, we'll get back to you on the details." But without a return phone call, I haven't been able share any more than what I learned from the following people who have actually investigated the old homestead.

Tim Ellison from Dead Serious Paranormal investigated the Sawyer Homestead and shared his story with me:

> *At the time there were four of us. Two investigators were upstairs near the cupola. Joe and I were on the first floor, but I can't remember the name of the room. Joe and I were doing some EVP work. We'd seen this cool little trick on* Ghost Adventures *where two people try to capture EVPs at the same time, then one person stops the recording and does a live playback as the other is still recording. I guess it's to see if we can capture EVPs live. So, we were in this room doing this live EVP session, and the doorknob started to shake really fast, as if someone was trying to open the door but it was locked. Since I was the closest to the door, I opened it really fast, and nothing was there. I did it quickly so if someone was messing with us, we would be able to catch them running away, but I didn't see anyone. That's the only unexplained experience I had at the Sawyer House.*

Two people visited the Sawyer Homestead for four hours in 2018 and experienced battery drain and a shadow figure they were unable to capture on film. So, the jury is still out. Feel free to contact me if you have personal experiences to share about this location.

CHAPTER 13

TURTLE ISLAND

In the mouth of Maumee Bay, about four and a half miles from the shores of both Lucas County, Ohio, and Monroe County, Michigan, sits a tiny piece of land by the name of Turtle Island. At one time, long ago, the island was over six acres, but storm erosion has caused it to shrink over the years. In the later part of the twentieth century, a decades-long dispute took place over the exact location of the Ohio-Michigan state line. The dispute wasn't completely settled until 1973, and both states jointly owned the one-and-a-half-acre island, straight down the center. As of today, the island is privately owned.

The earliest known inhabitants of Turtle Island were the Miami Indians. The island is said to have been named for the Miami chief Little Turtle, one of the signers of the Greenville treaty. By 1794, British troops had built a fort on the island, which they were using to end United States general Anthony Wayne's conquest of the Northwest Territory. They didn't succeed, and the fort was soon abandoned. In the years to come, the island would be used for a wide range of purposes, from housing for American soldiers to a yacht club that held races from the island northward.

In 1827, the island was sold at a federal government auction in Monroe, Michigan; then, in 1831, Edward Bissel of Lockport, New York, sold the island back to the government for $300. It was at that time that the first lighthouse was built on the island. It had eight reflectors and lamps. The number of lamps, and thus amount of oil required, fluctuated periodically. The forty-five-foot-square tower, a yellow brick keeper's quarters and an oil house stood on the island. It wasn't until 1832 that the first lightkeeper position was filled by William Wilson. It only took a couple of years for the lighthouse foundation to begin deteriorating; in 1834, $2,000 was secured to make a better foundation for the light. The foundation was redone again in 1837, 1838 and 1866.

On July 18, 1837, Captain Wilkinson, the superintendent of the public works at the lighthouse, was working on repairs when he was fatally injured by the hammer of a pile driver. It amputated his arm, broke both of his legs and fractured his skull.

Early in the nineteenth century, the continuous erosion to the island dropped the island size to two acres. As a result, in 1839, five hundred cubic yards of soil was brought to the island to expand its surface area. In subsequent years, both soil and stone were brought to the small island; the efforts were not enough, and the island continued to dwindle down to today's size—under one and a half acres.

On November 20, 1845, lighthouse inspector John McReynold gave a report on the Turtle Island Light: "This light is kept by an old bachelor

Turtle Island Lighthouse with the attached keeper's house. This photo was taken in 1885. The 561-foot retaining wall is visible in the forefront of the photograph. *Courtesy of U.S. Lighthouse Society Archives.*

who takes great pride in keeping his apparatus in good order, and on which all his affection seems to rest. This light is an important one, no repairs necessary."

The *Detroit News Press* stated that in 1853, lightkeeper Okey McCormick was appointed, replacing Gordon S. Wilson. Gordon was the principal lighthouse keeper from 1850 to 1853 and was paid $400 a year. After being dismissed from Turtle Island, he went on to keep other lighthouses like Horseshoe Reef Light from 1875 until 1881.

Here is a comprehensive list of Turtle Island lightkeepers, according to the Clifford Lighthouse Research Catalog:

William Wilson, Principal Lighthouse Keeper (1832–32)
Ben Cass, Principal Lighthouse Keeper (1832–33)
Samuel Choate, Principal Lighthouse Keeper (1833–34)
Benjamin I. Woodruff, Principal Lighthouse Keeper (1834–35)
Oliver Whitmore, Principal Lighthouse Keeper (1835–37)
Ebenezer Ward, Principal Lighthouse Keeper (1837–39)
Gideon L. Kelsey, Principal Lighthouse Keeper (1839–47)
Alexander H. Cromwell, Principal Lighthouse Keeper (1847–50)
Gordon S. Wilson, Principal Lighthouse Keeper (1850–53)
Okey McCormick, Principal Lighthouse Keeper (1853–54)
Isaac McCormick, Principal Lighthouse Keeper (1854–58)
James Coonahan, Principal Lighthouse Keeper (1858–61)
Andrew Harrison, Principal Lighthouse Keeper (1861–67)
Nathan W. Edson, Principal Lighthouse Keeper (1867–69)
Ann M. Edson, Principal Lighthouse Keeper (1869–72)
Samuel Jacobs, Principal Lighthouse Keeper (1872–74)
Emmett A. Root, Principal Lighthouse Keeper (1874–75)
William I. Haynes, Principal Lighthouse Keeper (1875–1904)
Guy McCormick, First Assistant Lighthouse Keeper (1855–59)
Michael Coonahan, First Assistant Lighthouse Keeper (1859–63)
Allen Harrison, First Assistant Lighthouse Keeper (1863–67)
William E. Burrows, First Assistant Lighthouse Keeper (1871–72)
Clara Jacobs, First Assistant Lighthouse Keeper (1873–74)

In 1855, the lighthouse was refitted with a fountain lamp and one burner. Ten years later, an entirely new lighthouse was built. Seven steps led up to the square brick 50-foot tower on a high stone foundation. It was dressed with rectangular windows, and the light burned using coal. On June 25, 1866,

Joseph D. Palmer was contracted to build a coal wharf on Turtle Island. At that time, a brick two-story, five-room lightkeeper's house was built, attached to the lighthouse. During the following years, a cistern, fog bell and well were added. In 1883, in further efforts to stop the erosion that threatened to carry away the entire island, the government built a 561-foot concrete retaining wall on the exposed shore. Since the time of the wall's construction, there has been negligible further erosion.

By the early twentieth century, Turtle Island's light was considered obsolete, after serving as a beacon of light for mariners for seventy-two years. On May 15, 1904, the lighthouse was permanently discontinued. Its lens was dismounted and, with the rest of the illuminating apparatus, was taken to the Maumee Bay Ranges Light Station to be shipped to the Buffalo Lighthouse Depot. The island was temporarily placed in the care of the keeper of the Maumee Bay Ranges Light Station.

At that time, the government decided to sell the island. On December 6, 1904, Turtle Island was sold at a public auction to A.H. Merrill of Toledo, Ohio, for $1,650. From there, the island changed hands several times. The Associated Yacht Clubs of Toledo leased the island from George L. Merrill in September 1935 for the purpose of establishing a yacht club and harbor of refuge.

There was a bump in the road, however, when the yachtsmen of Toledo, Sandusky, Detroit and Monroe—as well as other mariners—began protesting the removal of the Turtle Island Light. They believed the entrance into the straight channel would be dangerous without the Turtle light. Commander Garst and Captain Reiter of the lighthouse board hurried to investigate the matter. It was never resolved.

Through the last century and beyond, occurrences have taken place on the island that have been deemed…suspicious—hauntingly so.

In December 1898, the *Detroit Free Press* published a short article teasing Lightkeeper Gibeaut; the article said Gibeaut was having pipe dreams, as he had seen a schooner wreck near the Turtle Island Light. Apparently, Franz Sigel and W.H. Dunham, both supposed to have been in the wreck, turned up at Benton Harbor unloading cargo off the boat. The month before, Gibeaut saw a small schooner go down just offshore with a crew of six men and one woman. He said it was close enough to him that he could see the small clipper loaded down with coal. He called for assistance at once, but upon reaching the island, no boat was found in distress. His sightings weren't limited to just floundering boats—the lightkeeper also claimed to have seen a partially bald Native American wearing a fur cape. Once again, he was ridiculed. Gibeaut had had enough. He left his post at the island, never completing his tenure as the Turtle Island lightkeeper.

Historical newspapers depict scores of boats sinking around Turtle Island, as well as several drownings. One such notable example is John Palmer, who drowned when his vessel called *Susquehanna* went down at Turtle Island.

Over the past two hundred years, dozens upon dozens of boats have sunk, capsized and had mechanical problems in the vicinity of the island. Is it a curse? Could Gibeaut be seeing phantom boats—visions of cursed boats?

In November 1949, two Michigan men, Robert O. Brown and Orville Volker, were experiencing quite a frustrating time at Turtle Island. They decided to go fishing from their boat near the island. The men weren't there but an hour when their boat stalled as they got closer to the island. They had to call the coast guard to tow them. Miraculously, the schooner started right up when they were just a mile from shore. Two weeks later, they decided to go out again. But on the second trip near Turtle Island, their boat capsized. They managed to stay afloat for an hour until the police pulled them from the water and had them sent to Riverside Hospital to be evaluated for exposure. Both times, the men summoned help by firing their shotguns. Later, after being released, Volker admitted that at the time of the capsize,

Turtle Island Lighthouse, taken in 2014. *Courtesy of U.S. Lighthouse Society Archives.*

they'd spotted a dark-skinned man wearing a fur blanket on the shore; the pair had thought perhaps he was stranded, as there were no boats at the dock. After capsizing, they'd soon forgotten all about the unknown man.

All through the twentieth century, explorers and young lovers reported seeing mysterious things on the island. Trespassers would run back to their boats after getting goosebumps. Among the instances reported have been shadowy figures and floating lights, attributed to former lightkeepers walking about the property with a lantern. Others continued to see the Native American who—by all accounts—fits the description of Chief Little Turtle. A few visitors have reported seeing a limping man without an arm traipsing across the brush toward the lighthouse. Others have spotted an apparition of a dog—the pet of a former lightkeeper.

James Arvanitis received Turtle Island in the mid-1960s as payment on a business debt. He tried to sell it ever since acquiring the island, but because of the rumors of hauntings, he had great difficulty selling the property. Perhaps it was the asking price—$40,000. The island was said to need $10,000 in estimated repairs. One will never know.

Since 1995, the island has been owned by Jim Neumann. Only remnants of previous structures exist, including the partial remains of the 1866 lighthouse. Neumann still has dreams of renovating the lighthouse. The dream has thus far not come to be, but he does have hope that his son will one day take on the task.

As a reminder—Turtle Island is privately owned and is closed to the public. That of course doesn't stop one from boating nearby; just be careful you don't capsize, sink or fall victim to any other slew of disasters.

CHAPTER 14

BOYSVILLE JUVENILE DETENTION CENTER

bandoned and crumbling, the remnants of the Boysville Juvenile
Detention Center lie off a semi-rural road lined with farmland,
woods and quiet homes in Monroe County's Frenchtown Township.
The main facility sits back far off the road, hidden from sight, unless one
knows exactly where to look. It was once an ideal location for young boys
trying to reset their lives. Some would say a few linger still in the run-down
building of the center.

In 1950, the Verona Fathers of the Comboni Missionaries of the Heart
of Jesus purchased the sixty-acre property for the purpose of constructing
a facility to train and educate future Comboni missionaries. The site would
also serve as the administrative offices for the missionaries, whose mission
it was to work with the poor and the "most abandoned" peoples around
the world.

According to a 2017 article in the *Monroe News*, Boysville of Michigan
purchased the property from the Verona Fathers in the late 1980s. Boysville
was an organization started by the Brothers of Holy Cross, the order
responsible for operating Monroe Catholic Central from the time of its
founding in 1944 until its merger with St. Mary Academy in 1986.

Boysville—later known as Holy Cross Children's Services–Moreau Center—
provided a private educational and housing alternative to incarceration for
troubled and delinquent youth in grades seven through twelve. The property,
which is situated at the intersection of Nadeau Road and Comboni Way,
included a forty-thousand-square-foot building. It housed a gymnasium, a

chapel, classrooms, a full-service kitchen, offices and a dormitory. The property also contained basketball courts and tennis courts.

Unfortunately, given the school-like nature of the facility—without fences or locked doors—many residents managed to escape. The fugitive boys would invariably get into trouble; they'd end up stealing vehicles or breaking and entering into nearby homes. In one case, a boy stole a jeep from a neighboring property and then drove to a bakery, where he killed one man and shot a twenty-four-year-old mother, paralyzing her. The young man ended up with a life sentence for his crimes.

After new security features were implemented to help protect nearby residents, the detention home and school continued to be operational until its primary source of funding—state grants from the Michigan Department of Human Services—was eliminated in 2008. The number of students able to be accommodated rapidly declined, and the facility was forced to close.

By 2010, the property was owned by the Michigan Catholic Conference, but it still sat unused. In 2017, the former Holy Cross Children's Services Center was donated to the St. Mary Catholic Central Endowment Fund. The SMCC Endowment Fund is a not-for-profit, private, charitable foundation whose purpose is to support Catholic secondary education in the Monroe area. Despite this change of hands, the building remained unused and continued to fall into serious disrepair. As of today, the former center remains abandoned and has become a magnet for ghost hunters, explorers, the homeless and—unfortunately—drug users. It's alleged to be haunted by past missionaries, former students and even some drug-addicted persons who sadly passed away after overdosing in the abandoned building.

But the reported paranormal activity began long before the school closed its doors for good. During the last few decades that the school was operational, students reported oddities such as doors slamming when no one was near.

The high school years, alternative or otherwise, are often both some of the best times in a young person's life as well as some of the worst. The intensity of this period and the oft-conflicting feelings experienced have a way of leaving a haunted impression behind.

While completing my research for this book, I received an anonymous personal account for this chapter:

> *I made my way through the woods with my dogs and contemplated about going inside. Curiosity won out. I'm an explorer by heart and I certainly wasn't prepared for the paranormal aspect. I was walking along a long*

dirty hallway when I heard the distinct sound of laughter. Okay, who could that be? There must be someone else exploring. I looked around inside and then went back outside and looked around…nothing, no one at all. I shrugged it off and went back in.

By the way, my dogs wouldn't go in the building with me; they kept sniffing around the outside and marking their territory so to speak.

I continued back down the long hallway, peeking into the rooms I came across. I heard the laughter again and a light banging noise. I sucked it up and just kept going, when I walked into this huge room, it appeared to be a classroom. Suddenly, my dogs outside begin barking. I could see slivers of sunlight coming in through the gaps in the wall and those gaps blacked out as if someone was outside walking past.

I said hello pretty loudly and asked if anyone was there. I got no response. I started to get a little creeped out. When I looked away from the wall toward the doorway that led back into the hallway I began hearing the bang, bang again, I turned to look, I saw a book on the ground that wasn't there before, I had just walked through there. I started heading for the door fast and that's when the banging started again repetitively. I heard the laughter again. I had had enough! I ran for the way out as the laughing and banging got louder. I didn't look back; my barking dogs and I ran off into the woods headed back home.

Who was laughing and banging in the abandoned school? Was it one of the juvenile inmates who used to walk the halls? Maybe a few of them playing a practical joke on the unsuspecting explorer?

Prospecting ghost hunters have reported paranormal experiences such as being touched about their shoulders and arms. Others have also reported sounds of laughter. EMF spikes are a regular thing in this old abandoned building and the desolate land surrounding it—even though the property is now without electricity. Strange EVPs have been recorded of an old lady asking, "Are you okay?" and saying, "Hello" and "young man."

After doing some research, I may have found why an older woman would be at a boys' detention home and school. During the late 1980s and throughout the 1990s, two older ladies, Hazel Miller and Mary Openkiowski, were resident "grandmas" for the young inmates. The two women were a part of the Foster Grandparent Program that operated out of the Monroe County Intermediate School District. They provided a role that was not authoritative but rather loving and kind, as a grandmother should be. The system worked for years until the facility closed. The women were interviewed for the *Battle Creek Enquirer*. "We've never felt afraid of the boys," said Miller, sixty-four years old at the time. Openkiowski, eighty-six years old and a retired nurse, also had her say: "I would just love to see anybody even shove me, the boys would be there right quick." Each morning while the school was operational, the article explained, both women would read to the students and help them with their homework. Sometimes they shared stories of setbacks that they themselves once faced as children, in hopes of making a connection with the students who were struggling. In each other, the boys and older women felt they had family. The article concluded with Openkiowski insisting, "They are my family!"

Could Mary Openkiowski still be lingering within the abandoned structure's walls, helping the boys with their schoolwork and reading to them?

This location is not open for ghost hunts or investigations. It is dangerous and illegal to trespass here, and serious danger lurks. At the time of the completion of this chapter, a twenty-three-year-old woman had just been found murdered inside the building. So, please enjoy the story but stay home.

CHAPTER 15

TERRITORIAL PARK

NAVARRE TRADING HOUSE

The Navarre Trading House complex is a restored historic French Canadian homestead along the River Raisin. The main building, erected in the late eighteenth century, is widely considered to be the oldest standing wooden residence in Michigan. It is the most complete example of French Canadian *piece-sur-piece* construction in the Old Northwest. Within the modern era, the house has been meticulously returned to how it would have appeared in the year 1797. Other buildings within Territorial Park include an 1810 cookhouse and a replica of a 1790s French Canadian–style barn.

In an article found in *Michigan History*, "Standing for Two Centuries: The Navarre-Anderson Trading Post," Dennis Au delineates the early history of the trading post, first constructed by François-Marie Navarre in 1789. Navarre was born in Detroit in the mid-eighteenth century, the son of Robert and Marie Barrois Navarre. In 1789, Navarre set up a trading post along the River Raisin near present-day Monroe. About nine years after marrying and beginning a family, Navarre renovated his trading post into a frontier home and brought his family to the site to live. Navarre added windows, an additional door and two room partitions. For the next five years, the Navarres and their nine children resided at the post on the fast-growing French Canadian settlement.

Under the wood slat siding sits a 1797 log cabin that was once the Navarre-Anderson Trading Post. *Photo by Samuel D. Holland, 2020.*

In the 1790s, Au writes, a man named John Anderson was hired by fur trader and merchant John Askin to set up a trading post on the Maumee River. Anderson arrived at the River Raisin in 1802 and decided to go into business for himself. John Anderson purchased the trading post house from François-Marie almost immediately after arriving. He owned the house until 1804, when he sold it to a Dr. Joseph Dazet and built a bigger house next door for himself and his family. That new home, however, was destroyed during the Frenchtown Massacre on January 23, 1813. Anderson's family moved back to the original trading post turned home in 1816, and they lived there until they could rebuild the home that had burned. The Anderson family kept the original trading post structure for many years, renting it out for extra income. John Anderson died in Monroe in 1840.

Au writes that Dr. Joseph Dazet and his wife, Catherine, to whom Anderson had sold the trading post in 1804 before ultimately buying it back again in 1816, were refugees of the French Revolution. They first settled in Gallipolis, Ohio, with other Frenchmen. By 1804, the couple had found their way to the River Raisin, where Dazet became the first physician in the region; he remained a favorite of the French habitants. There is no written record of what happened at the doctor's house during the Battle of the River Raisin, but the bullet holes that riddle all four façades of the trading post remain a testimony to those violent days. The Dazets stayed in the newly renamed town of Monroe until approximately 1830, when they moved to Detroit.

According to Au, John Anderson once again purchased the old trading post in 1830 and then sold it in 1835. He writes that the post passed through

A view of the Plexiglas window in the west side of the Navarre-Anderson Trading Post that enables one to view not only a portion of the original log cabin structure but also expended musket balls and buckshot from the Battles of the River Raisin that are embedded in the wood. *Photo by Jeri Holland, 2020.*

several owners until 1857, when Israel Ilgenfritz purchased the plot. The Ilgenfritz family became prominent Monroe nurserymen; ultimately, the family would enjoy an eighty-six-year tenure of the property. To preserve the house, the Ilgenfritz family moved it from its original location on Elm Avenue in Monroe in 1894.

In 1943, the Ilgenfritz family sold the trading post building to Bud Haddix, who in turn sold it to Roger Russeau and Peter Navarre in 1969. According to Au, Russeau and Navarre planned to raze the building to expand a parking lot but were hesitant about destroying a building of rumored historical significance. Russeau and Navarre then reportedly contacted Matthew C. Switlik, director of the Monroe County Historical Museum, and asked him to delve into the importance of the building. Switlik's investigation revealed the building's architectural and historical heritage. The Monroe County Historical Society moved it to its present-day location in 1972 and has restored it as a French homestead.

To learn more in depth about the Navarre-Anderson Trading Post, read *The Navarre Cabin: A Study in Pièce sur Pièce Construction* by Jeffrey L. Green.

PAPERMILL SCHOOL

Papermill School was erected in the late 1860s. It is said to have been named after the former Christopher McDowell Papermill, which once operated about one hundred yards upriver. The schoolhouse served Raisinville and Frenchtown Townships, grades kindergarten through eight, until 1962. After its time as a schoolhouse came to an end, the building was the site of the Monroe County Museum's Martha Barker Country Store Exhibit for several decades. Several years ago, renovations began to turn the Papermill School into a visitors' center for the site.

The Monroe County Museum's website depicts the interesting history of the school. Originally, the building was equipped with a wood-burning stove, pump water from the well and a single communal dipper. The room boasts large windows on either side, but for overcast days or for occasional evening school or community events, illumination was supplied by kerosene lanterns. Typical outhouses were available outside the building.

According to the Monroe County Museum, a wooden bridge that spanned the river at this location was destroyed by a flooded River Raisin in 1887. From that time until 1967, there was no bridge to allow people to cross the river at the site. Students residing on the south bank of the river often came to school by boat, while others walked to school through thick spring mud and deep winter snows or took advantage of a frozen river to skate to school.

In 1955, the museum states, Papermill became a part of Monroe Public Schools, and the schoolhouse was reduced to just third-grade students. By 1962, the nearby Raisinville Elementary School had been built and Papermill School was closed. From 1969 to 2018, the school building housed the Martha Barker Country Store Exhibit, which was named in honor of the woman whose committee worked for five years to create this new museum.

With history this deep, do you have any doubt there's something lingering within Territorial Park?

I felt it important to include the names of those who lived within the walls of the cabin because there have been a few accounts where ghost hunters have managed to capture class-A EVPs in Territorial Park. During the day—and the dark of night—people have been amazed to record key words like "fur," "river" and the mind-boggling "François" and "Peter."

Tim Rehahn went to the site with a few friends from his Spirit World Paranormal Investigations team. It was a quiet midday, and no one was around when they decided to take a walk through the trading post and grounds. When the group spotted someone watching them through a

Left: Erected in the late 1860s, the Papermill School was named for the McDowell Paper Mill. *Photo by Samuel D. Holland.*

Right: The Country Store Museum was once housed in the old rural school building called the Papermill School. *Photo by Samuel D. Holland.*

Undated historic view of Papermill School. *Courtesy of James Wasarovich.*

window, a couple investigators went in to ask a tour guide some questions. They didn't find anyone. While inside, Tim sat on the steps. Suddenly, someone knocked on the door behind him. He opened it, but yet again, no one was around. Those inside the cabin thought Tim made the knocking sound, and Tim thought they had done it.

I contacted the director of the Monroe County Museum, and this is the response I received:

> *Thank you for your interest in considering our site in your book,* Haunted Monroe. *We are approached about our various sites being haunted with a degree of frequency. As we feel claims of hauntings can distract from the actual history of a location and potentially spread misinformation about the people that lived and worked in our historic structures, the Monroe County Museum System declines to participate.*
>
> *Museum staff and volunteers have decades of experience working in our buildings in a wide range of daytime and nighttime hours. Though we offer programs based upon the legends and lore of our community, we make no claims nor promote the idea that our sites are haunted. Because, simply stated, they are not.*
>
> *I realize some historical organizations embrace haunted history or promote it as a means to generate interest and visitation. We maintain that our long-term responsibility to historical fact overrides any short-term gains.*

I believe, tried and true, that history and ghosts go hand in hand. Territorial Park certainly has the history—so is it haunted?

Spirit World Paranormal Investigations thinks so. And so do I.

CHAPTER 16

HULL'S TRACE

Governor William Hull was an admired American soldier and politician. An American Revolutionary War veteran, Hull was appointed governor of Michigan Territory in 1805. He was then appointed general of the Northwest Army of the United States in the spring of 1812.

In April of that year, as the United States prepared for a possible war with Great Britain, Hull was ordered to prepare to invade Canada. Hull and his army traveled to Ohio and began their long march to Detroit. As they headed out with their supply wagons, they found there wasn't an adequate road for them to cross through Ohio and into southeast Michigan. Thus, Hull's troops were forced to build a two-hundred-mile-long road as they headed north.

While Hull's army worked his way north building the road through Ohio's Great Black Swamp, Captain Herbert Lacroix's men, from the Michigan Militia, were building a road as well, following the ancient Shore Indian Trail from Detroit south to the River Raisin.

The Shore Indian Trail served as one of several main land routes for early European settlers during Northwest expansion. The trail started at the rapids of the Maumee River and eventually passed through Monroe before moving on toward Detroit.

The men had only basic tools and not many horses, so the work was difficult. Every wet or swampy area had to be corduroyed, which entailed laying logs parallel to each other and perpendicular to the road. These logs were then covered with dirt in order to fill the gaps and make the roadway smooth.

On June 18, 1812, war was declared. By July 5, Lacroix's unit had reached the Huron River and Hull's army had reached Michigan Territory. The road Hull's men had laid was referred to as Hull's Trace.

Bay Settlement of Monroe County, Michigan by Lambert M. LaVoy gives a detailed account of the route. The following is as it appears in the book:

> *The Hull Road entered Michigan from Maumee from a point where it crossed Halfway Creek near Livi Morin's residence (now Suder Ave.) then angling northward and a little to the east of Suder Avenue to a point east of the Charles Dohm residence (Vienna Road) running parallel to the now Penn Central Rail Road to Bay Creek. After crossing the creek, the road curved northward entering the Bay Woods (on Erie Road east of the buildings of the Benore farm), continued north across the farm of Leo Labardee, (Lakeside Road) a little to the east of the buildings… and on to Otter Creek over a bridge not far from east of LaSalle. The Hull Road then slowly curved North east to the vicinity of LaPlaisance Road and ends at E. Albain Road. Hull road is still in existence in Monroe County. It runs north from LaPlaisance Road and ends at E. Albain Road. (By traveling south on Kentucky avenue to Albain road jogging a half a mile eastward, then south on Hull road, one retraces the trail taken by the fleeing Kentuckians at the battle of the River Raisin.) General Hull's trail ran northward on Kentucky Ave. to E. Front St. and east on block to Winchester St. and then north crossing the River Raisin in the vicinity of the Winchester St. bridge and northward on the Dixie Highway towards Detroit.*

The following winter, Hull's Trace was utilized by American soldiers to reach Frenchtown (present-day Monroe). There, the Americans were brutally beaten by the British and Native Americans during two short battles that took place on January 18 and 22. On January 23, the remaining wounded were attacked again by drunken renegade Indians. Those Americans who weren't slaughtered on the twenty-third were marched northward by the renegades on Hull's Trace, the present-day North Dixie Highway.

It was on this route that even more Americans were tortured and assassinated.

Afterward, Lieutenant Baker of the Second United States Regiment gave the following account describing his journey along Hull's Trace:

On the morning of the 22ⁿᵈ of January, I was captured by the Indians, about 9 o'clock, with another officer and about 40 men. Closely pursued by an overwhelming force of Indians, were endeavoring to affect our escape, and had attained a distance of about three miles from Frenchtown, when an offer of quarter was made by the Indian chief [a person who is given quarter is given leeway and not treated harshly]. *Many Indians on horseback being in our front and flanks, four or five hundred in our rear, tomahawking the hindmost, and withal the men being very much wearied with running through deep snow, we concluded it best to accept the chief's proposition. Accordingly, we assembled around him, and gave up the few remaining arms that were still retained in the flight. In a few minutes the Indians on foot came up, and notwithstanding the chief appeared solicitous to save, massacred about half of our number. I was led back towards the river along the road we had retreated in. The dead bodies of my fellow comrades, scalped, tomahawked and stripped, presented a most horrid spectacle to my view. I was at length taken to a fire near Colonel Proctor, where I remained till our army capitulated, and marched by me towards* [Fort] *Malden* [Ontario]. *Major Madison, as he was marching past on the road, demanded me of the British officer commanding the guard, as an American officer; but the noble Briton replied with a sneer, "you have too many officers," and ordered the column to advance, which had made a partial halt. I was taken to Sandy creek, about three miles off, on Hull's road, and there kept for the night with about 20 other surviving prisoners. Next morning my master left me in charge of an old Indian, and with the exception of 20 or 30, all the Indians in the camp went back towards the River Raisin. They returned about two o'clock, P.M. bringing a number of fresh scalps and about 30 more prisoners, many of whom were wounded, though with a single exception, none dangerously. I was told by the prisoners that the Indians had that morning returned to the village* [Frenchtown], *and massacred Captain Hickman and a great many others, and that they were fearful Major Graves and Captain Hart were of the number; that some of the wounded had been scalped alive and burnt in the houses. I was scarcely told the* [details of the massacre of Frenchtown] *when a* [man] *who was standing by my side, was knocked down, scalped and afterwards tomahawked. Three others were successively treated in the same manner.*

Lieutenant Baker was held in Windsor, Canada, for a month. While there, he was told that in addition to the soldiers and Frenchtown citizens killed during the massacre, another sixty men were scalped and tomahawked on Hull's Trace on their journey through present-day Monroe County. As a prisoner of war, he continued to see more gruesome scenes:

Judge Woodward has ascertained several instances of great barbarity exercised on our prisoners. Massacres were not only committed on the 22ⁿᵈ and 23ʳᵈ but also on the 24ᵗʰ, 25ᵗʰ, and 26ᵗʰ and three weeks afterwards fresh scalps were brought along Hulls road to [Fort] Maden. Should this relation be doubted, many living witnesses of high standing for probity, may be found to attest them.

After the War of 1812, the floodgates of western expansion fully opened. Hull's Trace was extensively used by early settlers traveling into Michigan Territory. The road north of River Raisin later became part of the Dixie Highway system. It was used by Ohioans and others seeking employment in the factories of Detroit.

The brutal tragedies that occurred along Hull's Trace surely left an imprint immediately south of River Raisin by the retreating American soldiers, as well as north of River Raisin continuing toward Detroit.

According to an oft-repeated claim, American soldiers can be seen from time to time limping across the road before disappearing. Recently, a man on his way home from working a late-night shift was stopped at the light at North Dixie Highway and Sandy Creek Road. It was quiet with one other car stopped at the light opposite him. He suddenly heard what sounded like several people rushing his car and shouting. Every hair on his body stood on edge. The sound stopped nearly as fast as it had begun. The light changed, and the local man sped away. He wasn't afraid to admit he greatly exceeded the speed limit the rest of the way home.

These are the only paranormal accounts pertinent to Hull's Trace that I could obtain. I challenge my fellow paranormal seekers to explore the original Hull's Trace and gather evidence. You just may see apparitions of wounded American soldiers trudging through deep snow or capture some EVPs explaining who they are and how they died. Perhaps someone can direct them home, where there is no pain and suffering.

CHAPTER 17

ROSELAWN CEMETERY

Matilda Knapp grew up with two sisters and five brothers on a farm in Raisinville, Michigan, in the latter part of the nineteenth century. In 1906, Matilda married a Monroe man by the name of Eugene Betz. Betz would serve several prominent roles in Monroe during his life, including that of Monroe county clerk and mayor. Before long, the two had become parents to a son and daughter. After a period of time, Matilda's father, Frederick, a survivor of the Battle of Gettysburg, experienced the death of his second wife. At that time, he came to live with Matilda and her husband on West Elm in Monroe. Before Frederick Knapp's death, he willed his farm to Matilda. However, Matilda passed before her father. She died on April 8, 1927, age forty-five, from complications relating to cholelithiasis. Frederick died on September 8, 1927, leaving the farm to Eugene. During her lifetime, Matilda had expressed her wish to be buried on her family's farm. Despite making this desire known, she was ultimately buried in Woodland Cemetery.

After the deaths of his wife and father-in-law, Eugene Betz, by then mayor of Monroe and president of the Consolidated Paper Company, inherited the Knapp farm. Betz wasn't quite sure what to do with his newly acquired farm, which was nonoperational and sitting in the middle of nowhere. A friend of Betz's suggested making the farm into a cemetery, pointing out that Woodland Cemetery would someday invariably run out of room. Betz went for the idea.

Roselawn Memorial Park was thus established in 1928 on the fifty-four-acre Betz farm. Betz hired a premier landscape architect from Washington,

D.C., to design the grounds and buildings. Betz's very first task was to have his wife reburied at Roselawn, fulfilling her request to be buried on the farm. On May 29, 1929, a man named William Amendt was the very first public burial, followed by James Kinnear later that day.

In 1937, a Vermont white marble mausoleum was built, which included eight private family rooms of ten crypts each. Matilda's casket was moved a second time to the Betz Room in the mausoleum. It is said that the Betz family mausoleum contains some of the Betz family furniture—a small sofa and plant stand.

Over the last eighty years, there have been dozens of reported sightings of an apparition of a woman walking the cemetery in broad daylight, only to disappear a few minutes later. The following is one such account from Angie of "Hauntings in Monroe, Michigan":

This morning I was out at Roselawn cemetery. I had turned left on the main road and about halfway down before the first curve a lady was walking west towards S. Dixie in the cemetery as she looked like she was going to a specific grave. About 15 feet after I passed her, I got out of my car to go to my mom's grave and this lady was gone. Nowhere to be found. No other cars besides mine and the workers. She was wearing tan pants and a baby blue button-down blouse. I noticed how tidy her gray haired bun was on the top of her head. She never looked in my direction so I can't tell you what she looked like. I am pretty sure I saw a ghost/spirit. It was way too quick for her to vanish that fast. Even if she had somehow made her way through the fence onto South Dixie I still would have seen her. But she was gone.

Roselawn Cemetery is located at 13200 South Dixie Highway in La Salle. If you visit, keep an eye out for the ghostly woman. She seems to appear the most in the afternoon.

PART II
LEGENDS AND LORE

CHAPTER 18

CAMP LADY OF THE LAKE

Near Luna Pier in Monroe County, along a particularly eerie stretch of Lake Erie's shore, one can find all that remains of a lively summer camp abandoned decades ago—the remnants of Camp Lady of the Lake.

The history of the camp is quite interesting. It was extensively depicted in a March 2021 *Monroe News* article. In 1940, the Catholic Charities of the Diocese of Toledo opened a summer camp for orphans and underprivileged children from Toledo. The camp, spanning fifty-five acres, included half a mile of Lake Erie shoreline in Monroe County.

Camp Lady of the Lake operated for twenty-nine years. Originally, it was open only to youngsters from Toledo's St. Anthony's Orphanage, but a local need for summer camps resulted in the camp eventually opening its doors to all children. Each year, the camp provided a summer home for about three hundred children, boys ages seven to thirteen and girls ages seven to sixteen. According to a May 25, 1945 article in the *Catholic Chronicle*, the main objective of the camp was "to provide sunshine, fresh air and nourishing food for children in need of physical development." Local Catholics within the diocese sponsored children who might not otherwise have been able to attend.

The children enjoyed a variety of recreational activities under the supervision of the staff, which was composed of college students, seminarians, nuns and a priest. The latter conducted daily Mass. Each week, the campers were assigned various chores, from aiding in the kitchen to cleaning up after

GROTTO — CAMP LADY OF THE LAKE, ERIE, MICH.

Camp Lady of the Lake opened in 1940. *Postcard purchased by Jeri Holland.*

a herd of sheep that were raised at the camp. The camp included a lodge that housed the dining hall, recreation room, chapel, kitchen, toilets and showers. The property was divided into two sections—one for girls and one for boys, with each having their own beach area separate from the other. The youngest children resided in the dorm, while the other campers slept in large tents and, later, cabins.

Camp activities included swimming, boating, archery, BB gun shooting, sports, handicrafts, fishing, dramatics, nature hikes and evening campfires with skits. The dining hall was the center for many functions at the camp, from church to meals to plays to dances. Movies were shown as well.

The camp ultimately closed in 1969, for reasons not readily apparent. The property was then purchased by the Consumers Power Company. In 2008, the former camp and surrounding area became part of the Detroit River International Wildlife Refuge, which extends from the Detroit-Windsor corridor to southern Monroe County. Today, not much remains of the former Camp Lady of the Lake. The majority of the property has eroded into the lake, and part of it has turned to marshland.

THE LEGENDS

Several local legends have circulated for decades about Camp Lady of the Lake. Although the camp has been gone for many years, the lore of the area still draws visitors, me included.

One of the most prolific Camp Lady legends tells of a member of the camp staff who one night took a walk along the beach of Lake Erie. Returning to

Camp Lady of the Lake today. The fifty-five-acre camp is now overgrown and partially eroded into Lake Erie. *Photo by Jeri Holland, 2022.*

camp, she found the entire camp ablaze. After finding that all the children had perished in the fire, the distraught counselor took her own life.

Another legend asserts that the area is haunted by several children who were drowned in the lake—or otherwise murdered—by a set of infamous sisters, "Seaweed Mary" and "Seaweed Ellen." Allegedly, the lake sisters were invented by mischievous camp counselors to scare the impressionable children. It is even said the counselors would sometimes sneak into terrified children's cabins at night and leave seaweed behind as a sign that the sisters had paid a visit during the night.

The third story of lore pertains to a fifteen-year-old girl named Florence who is alleged to have fallen in love with an eighteen-year-old local boy just prior to World War II. The teenage couple was unable to marry prior to the young man going off to war; sadly, he was killed in action and would never return. Florence was said to have been in such distress over her lost love that she committed suicide in order to join him in death. There is more than one version of this legend; some say Florence committed suicide in the woods, while the others state she drowned herself in Lake Erie.

The Haunts

Visitors to the camp have reported hearing screaming children in the dead of night and seeing apparitions of ghostly figures, including that of a lone woman walking along the beach in the deep, murky darkness of the wee hours of the morning. Some visitors have even reported being chased by a frightening black form.

The 99.1 WFMK website shares three anonymous witness accounts:

Witness #1:
I went up there for two solid years and captured EVPs and photos and have seen things unexplainable by myself or friends. The "ghost" was a coherent soul that was evil and said he was going to kill us.

Witness #2:
As soon as we got in there, we started hearing things like what sounded like laughter…so we went deeper in.…That's when it started getting worse. We [saw] what looked like a little girl wearing a dress, but she was glowing white. Then we heard the twigs snapping all around us and the laughter again. That night I went to Lady of the Lake, a non-believer of ghosts and left a believer.

Witness #3:
Every time we go up to that beach something unexplained happens, and me
and my friend have many more stories about our experiences there as well as
pictures with many orbs seen in the pictures.

Usually, legends and lore are derived from a tiny grain of truth. However, I have found nothing to corroborate any of the "facts" pertaining to the legends associated with Camp Lady of the Lake.

I ventured to this area in 2020, and although I found the place hauntingly quiet and uncomfortable, I didn't capture any electronic voice phenomena or anything suspicious in my digital photos.

To visit the former Camp Lady of the Lake for yourself, take I-75 north to exit 5 (Erie Road) and head east. Continue until you reach the gate. If you walk past the gate down to the water, you may come across the old "Camp Lady of the Lake" sign.

CHAPTER 19
DOG LADY ISLAND

I f you've lived for any amount of time in Monroe County or its surrounding counties, you've no doubt heard the terrifying local legend of the Dog Lady and her island.

Officially named Kausler's Island, Dog Lady Island—as the locals refer to it—is located in Plum Creek, in the section that widens prior to merging into Lake Erie. The island can be reached by taking East Dunbar Road to a causeway that connects the island to the mainland.

According to the website "Legend Tripping Through Historic Monroe," the earliest records refer to the island as Fox Island. The island changed hands multiple times throughout the years. Fox Island was purchased by the Kausler family in the late 1800s and was sold to another private owner in the 1940s.

Michigan banned alcohol in 1918, two years before Prohibition took place nationwide. Undeterred, Michiganders found various ways to get their hands on alcohol. The state's location, a stone's throw from Canada, helped the effort immensely as rumrunners became quite popular. These boats, carrying wine, beer and liquor from Canada down throughout the Great Lakes, were known for their speed—the faster the boats, the quicker alcohol could be spread along the Great Lakes' coasts.

Providing seclusion, Dog Lady Island was a popular inlet for rumrunners. Local newspaper articles of the day told of the island's illegal activities and ties to Prohibition.

Kausler's Island/Dog Lady Island sits in Plum Creek. *Courtesy of Google Maps, 2023.*

On Christmas Eve 1925, the Michigan State Police and federal agents raided a roadhouse on Kausler's Island belonging to William Green of Monroe. The *Times Herald* reported the raid resulted in the confiscation of 9,600 bottles of Canadian beer.

In May 1927, the *Herald Press* reported that in a raid of a liquor cache on Kausler's Island, Michigan state troopers had seized 1,500 cases of Canadian beer, 60 cases of whiskey and two trucks. The contraband was destroyed, while the confiscated trucks were taken to the barracks of the troopers at South Rockwood. The cases of liquor and transport vehicles were valued at more than $1,200, or $20,500 in today's money.

Following Prohibition, the island again found itself in the news, this time for other reasons. In the 1930s, the city sent its garbage to a pig farm located on the island. According to a 1936 article in the *Times Herald*, local residents complained profusely about the smell that emanated from the pigs. The outcry was so severe that the wooden bridge leading to the island was dynamited, stopping the city garbage from making its way to the pigs—and therefore, stopping the swine from being fed.

Then, during the 1950s, the island became an infamous party spot for all ages. In fact, the May 1959 *Lansing State Journal* reported that many people had been arrested in what the publication referred to as a "Wild Orgy on Lake Isle." Thirty-one people, including many teenagers, were taken into custody after Mr. and Mrs. William Van Orsdale complained that several perpetrators had entered their home while they were sleeping. James Jacobs, Monroe Township's justice of the peace, even set up court right in the jail, the newspaper said, in order to handle the miscreants. Charges filed ranged from contributing alcohol to minors to possession of liquor and breaking and entering.

It's hard to pinpoint the original source of the Dog Lady legend, but it most likely began sometime in the 1960s. One would imagine the Prohibition-tied activities of the island and its alcohol-fueled parties of the '50s contributed to the lore that continued for decades.

So, who is the Dog Lady, you ask, and how did the island come to bear her name? The basics of the legend are largely agreed upon to go something like this. In 1961, a mansion on the island burned to the ground. Shortly afterward, the mansion's owner died. His widow, now alone, without a home and hopelessly distraught, aimlessly wandered the island, taking shelter among the run-down, abandoned buildings. Legend has it the woman was completely isolated, with the exception of a pack of wild dogs. This strange woman became known as the Dog Lady. As young adults visited for parties and then returned from the island, the legend only expanded and became more detailed.

The reclusive woman was alleged to have appeared when partiers gathered around their campfires, drinking and smoking. They often claimed to see her looking wild, in old-fashioned clothing, always in the presence of her savage pack of dogs. Most say she began to have more in common with her snarling dogs than she did with humans. Some accounts say the woman ran about on all fours, viciously tearing at the flesh of dead animal carcasses among her pack of dogs.

Somewhere along the line, the Dog Lady began to be described as tongueless. Whether her tongue was lost as the result of a run-in with the

Access to Kausler's Island/Dog Lady Island currently costs five dollars. *Photo by Melissa Owens.*

dogs or was from an attack by a biker gang called the Iron Caskets all depends on which story you read. The Dog Lady was also reported by witnesses to have been seen eating small animals—snarling, grunting and growling while doing so. Perhaps she lost her tongue while fighting over kills with the dogs.

One late twist to the urban legend was that the Dog Lady had a telephone. Proponents of this part of the story had somehow learned of her phone number; if you called it, supposedly Dog Lady herself would answer—with growls and barking, of course.

University of Toledo English professor and folklorist Dr. Daniel Compora shared with me his 2004 article from the FOAFTale News:

> *In some variations of the legend, Dog Lady remains alive, but supposedly sleeps in the coffin. Almost every variation of the story includes the coffin, undoubtedly because, when I visited the island in 1988, there was an object on the island that did resemble a coffin lid. Following an interview that I gave to the* Monroe Evening News *in 2006, I was contacted by someone who claimed to have worked at one of the local cemeteries who said the object was in fact a mausoleum lid, one of several which were brought to the island to help make a bridge for easier access.*

Legend has it the widow, alone and homeless, began to scare visitors to the island. Later, this version alleges, the Dog Lady was murdered by members of a motorcycle gang, the Iron Coffins. The Iron Coffins are an outlaw motorcycle club founded in Toledo, Ohio, in 1966.

The majority of urban legends usually begin with a shred of truth, so on the hunt I went for one. There is little to definitively attribute to the origins of the story, but one May 1930 article in the *Lansing State Journal* pertaining to the island's owner, George Kausler, caught my attention. Kausler died in 1930 of an unknown cause. The article read, "Owner of Island Dies. George Kausler, 74, owner of Kausler Island and a member of the old Monroe Light Guards, is dead. May 30th, 1930."

After delving into the world of Ancestry.com, it appears that George Kausler did leave a widow, Elizabeth. Mrs. Kausler continued living in Monroe, Michigan, until her death on July 1, 1944.

Could this woman, the widow of Mr. Kausler, be the lonely, disfigured woman who scared young people and drove them from her island before and after her death?

Despite her apparent demise at the hands of the Iron Coffins, stories of the Dog Lady haunting the island persist to this day.

CHAPTER 20
THE MONROE MONSTER

In the mid-1960s, Monroe locals began to talk about a large human-like creature living near Mentel Road, in the nearby woods by a farm and industrial area. By the summer of 1965, the Michigan State Police had checked into a rash of reports of the beast, described as towering, hairy and upright-walking. From June to August of that year alone, more than a dozen sightings were reported in Monroe County.

On the night of August 17, 1965, at approximately 11:30 p.m., a local mother and daughter were driving home toward Naseau Road, along a gravel road, when they alleged to have encountered the creature. "About 300 yards away, where the woods come close to the road, I saw something," Mrs. George Owens, thirty-eight at the time, later recalled in her account to the *Detroit Free Press*.

"I told Christine not to stop. But it was on us. I screamed and Christine screamed. I looked over at my daughter and there was this huge, hairy hand on top of her head," Mrs. Owens continued.

"He reached in and grabbed my hair!" added seventeen-year-old Christine Van Archer, who admitted to then losing control of the vehicle. The ladies reported the car then stalled. According to the women, the beast continued to cling to the side of the car with a grip on Christine's hair.

The teenager then stated that although she didn't remember much else after that, she did remember that the monster knocked her head against the car door moments before she fainted.

"I screamed for help until the monster disappeared," Mrs. Owens said.

Meanwhile, men from a nearby house heard screams, gathered up the women and took them back to Mrs. Owens's parents' house. It was there that Christine began developing a black eye from—as she alleged—having been knocked into the car door by the monster.

"I think it was more afraid of me than I was of it. I think it jumped on the car and its hand caught in my hair and it was simply trying to get loose. He was all hairy and the hairs were like quills. They pricked me whenever I touched them," Christine told the *Times Herald* out of Port Huron.

Mrs. Owens and her daughter subsequently lived in fear of the beast in the nearby swamp, just a half mile from their home.

The two women—and others—who had encountered the beast described it as a black monster, seven feet tall, with arms like logs and hair that was tough as wire obscuring its face. Witnesses said it howled, screamed and grunted, sometimes sounding like a woman, sometimes like a dog.

David Thomas, twenty-three, who resided on Dix Road at the time, was quoted in a local publication as having seen "the thing" while traveling on Nadeau Road a week prior, on August 11, 1965.

"Suddenly we saw this thing," Thomas told the reporter from the *Detroit Free Press*. "I thought it was a prankster trying to scare us. I jumped out of the car to see what it was. I took a swing at it but I couldn't reach it. It was at least three heads taller than me, and I'm six feet tall."

David Thomas later claimed to have found two hairs about an inch and a half long caught on the chrome strips of his car. "With a skull line an inch and a half deep, he must be some monster," Thomas reportedly told the local police at the time.

Following these sightings, the monster was next reportedly spotted in Frenchtown and Ash Townships, which forced the state police to release a statement on August 19, 1965, notifying the public that they were increasing patrols in the area.

Within days of the summer of 1965 sightings, crowds had begun flocking to Monroe. The monster, in fact, was the biggest public interest since the building of the atomic power plant a few years prior. Roads leading into the area were jammed. Business was booming at local restaurants, motels and service stations.

"They're coming from all over Michigan," police sergeant Howard Kuillin was quoted in local newspapers as saying.

The local authorities made it quite clear that they found the entire story absurd.

Then, on August 18, 1965, the *Times Herald* shared several incidents that had allegedly happened to those among the swarm of monster hunters. The first story to be published described an unnamed young girl who had shown up at the Monroe police station and presented red marks on her arm as proof that the now-infamous monster had dragged her. "Poison ivy!" a policeman on duty had declared before he escorted her out the front door of the police station. Others reported finding footprints of the beast and cornering it in the woods.

Not far from the sightings was the Enrico Fermi atomic power plant. Its gates required locks, and extra guards needed to be posted after members of a ragged vigilante band tramped over the power company's property in search of the monster. Several of the group were alleged to have said they believed the creature to be a nuclear mutation, spawned by the atomic plant.

George Spillson, who owned the Pixie Drive-In during this time, told the *Petoskey News-Review* on August 19, 1965, that he didn't care what the monster really was, just as long as it stayed around. "My carhops were a little perturbed by all the guns and baseball bats at first, but we're doing a Friday or Saturday night's business every day." The drive-in even began selling "monster burgers and shakes" to their customers.

But not all in Monroe County believed the tales of alleged run-ins with the Monroe Monster. By the end of the first week following their reported ordeal, Mrs. George Owens and her daughter Christine had seemingly tired of their sighting being challenged. The women proclaimed to everyone who doubted them that they'd be more than willing to submit to a lie detector test.

"I know what we saw is real and I don't like people thinking it's a hoax, that's why we agreed to do the lie test," Mrs. Owens told a reporter from the *Times Herald*.

Her daughter added, "Everyone who has seen the monster is willing to take the test. We'll pack their police headquarters wall-to-wall with people."

State police detective Patrick Lyons of the Flat Rock Post told the *Detroit Free Press*, "This thing has gone so far that we want to prove, once and for all, that there is no monster or discover exactly what it is that's out there."

Monroe County sheriff's workers refused to investigate reports of the monster any further but were forced to patrol Mentel Road to control crowds of monster hunters that gathered nightly.

The *Detroit Free Press*, which had followed the story from the beginning, published regular follow-ups throughout the summer.

On Monday, August 23, 1965, Mrs. George Owens and her daughter Christine Van Archer took and flunked a state police–administered polygraph. They were immediately critical of the test. Furthermore, the women shared with the public that a former judge from Fostoria, Ohio, James Ford, had given them a lie detector test after he was hired by the radio station WFOB. Station officials confirmed the test had been administered to the women by Ford, that he was a trained polygrapher and they had indeed passed the test.

Michigan State Police sergeant Frank Barkman, who had administered the first test, reportedly responded, "It is our opinion that they were lying."

"I know what I saw, and no one can change my mind," Christine said after Sergeant Barkman's statement was released. "I have seen the monster five times!"

Then, David Thomas came forward retracting his first account of the monster. He said he wanted to "clear up" part of his story.

"I knew it was a person with something like a fur coat drawn up over his head," confessed Thomas. "I could see regular pants legs. He never really did throw me anywhere."

And remember those two hairs allegedly found by David Thomas on his car? On September 1, 1965, they were determined by the Michigan State Police to belong to a paintbrush. Months later, Thomas confessed that his experience was a hoax.

Monroe Monster's biggest advocate, Mrs. George Owens, maintained she hadn't seen it since October 1965. State police detective Sergeant Patrick Lyons, who was later transferred to the Redford Post and promoted, called it a "figment of the imagination," as did the Monroe County sheriff and the trailer court owner where Mrs. Owens lived. But Mrs. Owens stuck to her guns: "A man from a big institution is working on proving the monster exists. He calls it a neo-giant. It takes fruit that we use as bait. The last time I saw it, it was crossing a field. Big and black with silver gray fur hanging down from its arms."

Bigfoot? Sasquatch? Some mutation stemming from the nearby nuclear plant? What could Monroe's monster be? Through the last one-hundred-plus years, there have been sightings of a giant, furry man-like creature across the expanse of Michigan and across the globe. But this one is right here at home. Have you seen the Monroe Monster?

PART III

OTHER RUMORED HAUNTS

PRETTY BOY FLOYD HIDEOUT

The Pretty Boy Floyd Hideout is located at 4408 Luna Pier Road on Lake Erie. On February 5, 1930, Charley "Pretty Boy" Floyd robbed the bank in Sylvania and was witnessed fleeing from the scene in a vehicle with Michigan license plates. From Ohio, Floyd fled over the border back into Michigan to his hideout.

Floyd was caught a couple of months later in Toledo, Ohio, and sentenced to twelve to fifteen years in the Columbus, Ohio State Penitentiary. On the train ride to Ohio to serve his sentence, Floyd jumped out the bathroom window of the moving train. He went on to rob banks for another four years.

The feds finally caught up to Floyd and killed him in Sprucevale (Calcutta), Ohio.

The Hideout has several accounts of possible hauntings. Vacationers have reported experiencing strange noises and doors opening on their own.

On May 20, 1930, Floyd was arrested by the Toledo, Ohio Police Department on a bank robbery charge and on November 24, 1930, he was sentenced to twelve to fifteen years in the Ohio State Penitentiary. *Courtesy of Heritage Sylvania.*

Right: Charles "Pretty Boy" Floyd teamed up with other outlaws to rob banks in Ohio, Michigan and Kentucky. This is the Farmers' & Merchants' Bank in Sylvania, Ohio, which they hit before escaping to Luna Pier, Michigan. *Courtesy of Heritage Sylvania.*

Below: Located in Luna Pier, this guesthouse was the actual home he hid out in after leaving the Toledo area. *Photo by Jeri Holland, 2022.*

The two-bedroom cottage has a 1930s speakeasy feel and is available to rent overnight. Booking can be done online.

CHATEAU LOUISE

The Chateau Louise is located in the small beachside town of Luna Pier. The building was originally a general store, built in 1894 and owned by a man named Paul Dussia. As of 1898, the general store was one of only five buildings in the town of Luna Pier, which, at that time, was a village called Lakeside.

Chateau Louise was once a meeting place for Toledo and Detroit gang members in the 1930s. *Photo by Jeri Holland, 2020, from Harold Drive.*

According to the "Michigan Cuisine" website and the *Monroe Evening News*, Dussia moved the location of his grocery store around the turn of the twentieth century. During that time, the grocery store included horse stalls, a small barn and guest rooms for weary travelers who wanted to visit the famous dancing pier. Early in its operation, Dussia leased his business to Mr. and Mrs. Sidney Baker. Sidney and his wife, Jesse, ran the store. Soon after, Jesse became the first postmistress in Michigan. The Bakers continued running the post office out of the store until Louise Geller purchased the building in 1934. Geller remodeled the structure and dubbed it the Chateau Louise. The Chateau Louise opened its doors to serve steaks, seafood—and alcohol. It was the very first business to obtain a fresh-off-Prohibition liquor license in the entire Lake Erie region.

Ultimately, Chateau Louise became a steady meet-up joint for gang members. It is now the oldest building in Luna Pier. Chateau Louise employees are more than happy to provide further history of the building along with stories of purported ghostly activity in the establishment. Chateau Louise is located at 4320 Luna Pier Road in Luna Pier.

SIDE TRACK SALOON

According to a 2018 *Monroe News* article, the building that now houses Monroe's Side Track Saloon was built in 1925. It originally served as the home of the former River Raisin Hotel, which had seven rooms available to rent. Later on, the establishment became the Moga family bar and then a taproom run by Pauline and Cecil Brannon. Most recently, the place was purchased by Doug Duvall and renamed the Side Track Saloon.

I stopped in one afternoon for a drink and asked about its haunted history. Doug Duvall's wife, Ellen, said that it was indeed haunted. She stated that objects move regularly, and various unexplained malfunctions occur more often than not. The building is located on the eastern side of the River Raisin battlefield. I'll leave it at that.

The Side Track Saloon is located at 1025 East Elm Street in Monroe.

THE MICHIGAN MUSEUM OF HORROR

The Michigan Museum of Horror's website boasts of a unique collection of real human skulls, including one that visitors can actually hold in their hands. The museum also houses real human skin, death photos of serial killer victims, horror films, caskets, bottles that held poison and much more horror memorabilia.

Given all the unique items in the museum, you just know it could be haunted. I gave them a call and asked, and it indeed is haunted. Mainly, a few of the upstairs display items have wreaked havoc in the building. But you'll have to visit yourself to find out more details. They host ghost hunts with equipment provided and regular tours for those who like the horror but want to leave the ghosts alone.

The museum is located at 44 South Monroe Street in Monroe. The website is www.natethompsonvideo.com.

DOTY CEMETERY

Doty Cemetery is located on North Custer Road in Ida, Raisinville Township. Once a family plot on the Joseph and Sarah True Doty farm, it now encompasses more than immediate family. The cemetery sits behind a farmhouse and is surrounded by a cornfield and woods. It boasts a desolate, haunting atmosphere that evokes goosebumps just by pulling down the path toward the graveyard.

Doty Cemetery sits in a cluster of woods surrounded by a cornfield. *Photo by Jeri Holland, 2020.*

Left: To access the cemetery, you have to drive down a grassy dirt path between two sprawling homes. Many of the graves on the outskirts of the lot are overgrown. *Photo by Jeri Holland, 2020.*

Right: Members of the John Roessler family were buried in Doty Cemetery in the 1920s. *Photo by Emily S. Holland.*

Frog Leg Inn

Frog Leg Inn is located at 2103 Manhattan Street in Erie. The structure that houses the inn was built in 1853. Located on the historic Dixie Highway, the building has a history as a bawdyhouse, speakeasy, schoolhouse and meat market. At one time, the inn was a prime spot for Prohibition-era bootleggers, just like other area restaurant gambling facilities in the region such as Northwood Villa and Chateau Louise.

In 1944, the inn was transformed by Tad and Catherine Cousino into a French-accented restaurant. Frog legs, prepared several different ways, are offered on the menu, of course. Other offerings include Lake Erie walleye, salmon, excellently broiled steaks and an unusual appetizer—deep-fried alligator.

The waitresses may offer up their experiences, should you stop for a good meal.

Frog Leg Inn was built in 1853. *Photo by Jeri Holland, 2022.*

BIBLIOGRAPHY

Ancestry. "Every Family Has a Story." www.ancestry.com.

Au, Dennis M. "Standing for Two Centuries: The Navarre-Anderson Trading Post." *Michigan History* 23, no. 6 (December 1989): 32–36. mlloyd. org/gen/navarre/text/mhnatp.htm.

Bertke, L.S. "Catholic Sumer Camps Served Underprivileged Boys and Girls." *Catholic Chronicle*, May 23, 2010.

Bulkley, J.M.C. *The History of Monroe County, Michigan*. Vol. 1. N.p.: Lewis Publishing Company, 1913.

City of Monroe. "Industry History." www.monroemi.gov.

Clift, G.G. *Remember the Raisin! Kentucky and Kentuckians in the Battles and Massacre at Frenchtown, Michigan Territory, in the War of 1812*. N.p.: Clearfield, 2002.

Compora, D.P. FOAFTale News. January 2014.

Dudley, T.P. *Battle and Massacre at Frenchtown, Michigan*. 1813.

Green, Jeffrey L. "The Navarre Cabin: A Study in Pièce Sur Pièce Construction." *International Society for Landscape, Place & Material Culture* 30, no. 1 (1998): 29–41.

LinkedIn. "Shore Indian Trail—Fort Miamis Trail—Hull's Trace." Thumbwind Publications, LLC. www.linkedin.com/company/thumbwind-publications.

Newspapers.com. Historical newspapers from 1700s–2000s. www. newspapers.com.

Rhode Island Republican. "Massacre at Frenchtown." April 1, 1813.

U.S. Lighthouse Society Archives. "U.S. Lighthouse Society Archives." uslhs. org/resources/finding_information/libraries_archives/uslhs-archives.

ABOUT THE AUTHOR

From family photos to important historical events about her hometown of Cuyahoga Falls, Ohio, Jeri Holland has dedicated passion, time, knowledge and immense effort in the pursuit of compiling and documenting the treasured past. She has created the website Cuyahoga Falls History (www.cuyahogafallshistory.com) and has joined the board in several historical societies, including the Cuyahoga Falls Historical Society as the president, vice president and secretary, to share this past with anyone who wishes to know it. Jeri has spearheaded community projects like the Cuyahoga Falls History Trail, the Haunted History Hike, history scavenger hunts and Underground Railroad tours.

Jeri has spent many hours studying firsthand what goes bump in the night, be it in the dark woods or run-down sanitariums and prisons. Jeri has also organized community events such as haunted scavenger hunts and hikes. Imparting the fact that the world is far more mysterious than what we see and hear every day is Jeri's goal; the goosebumps aren't bad either.